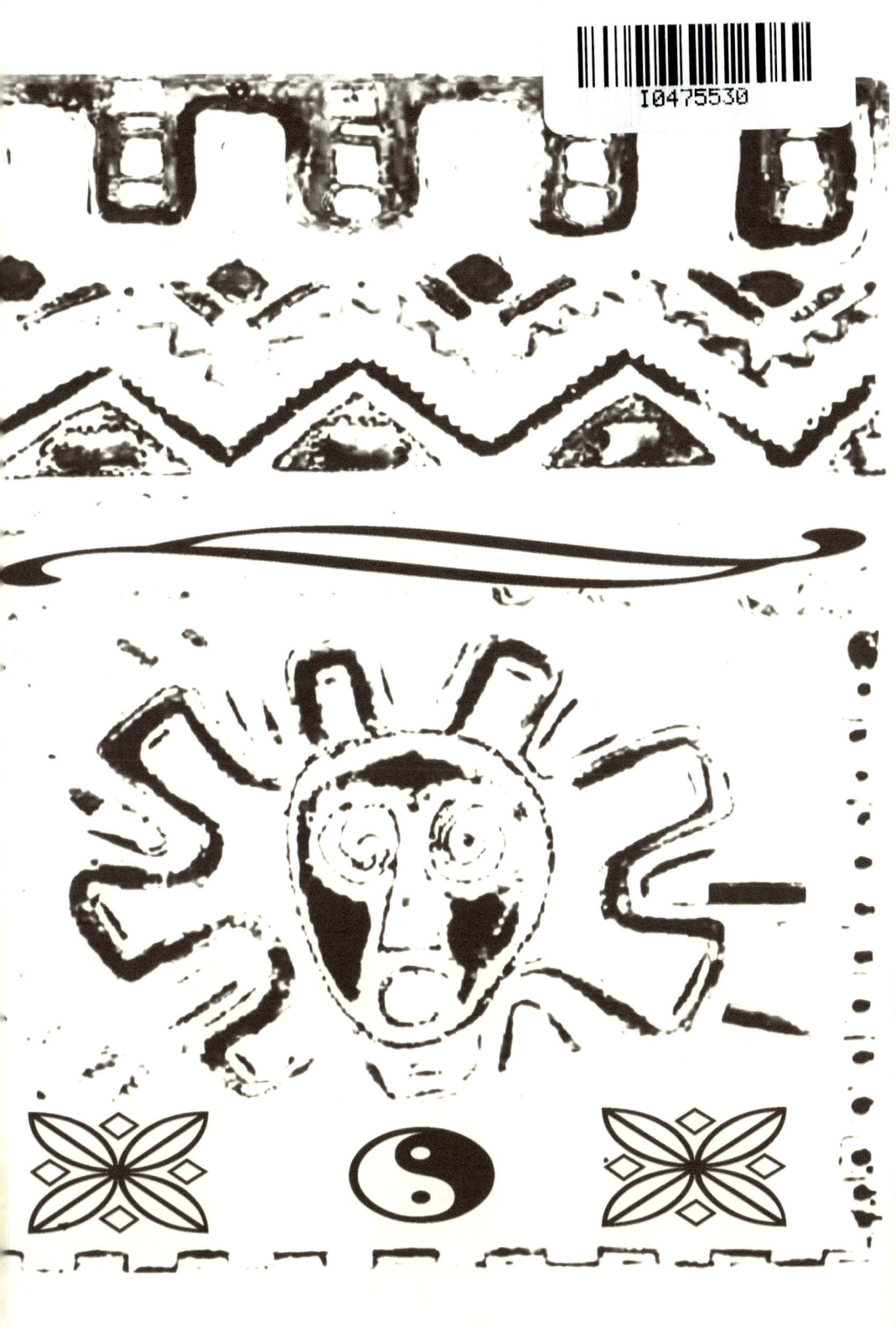

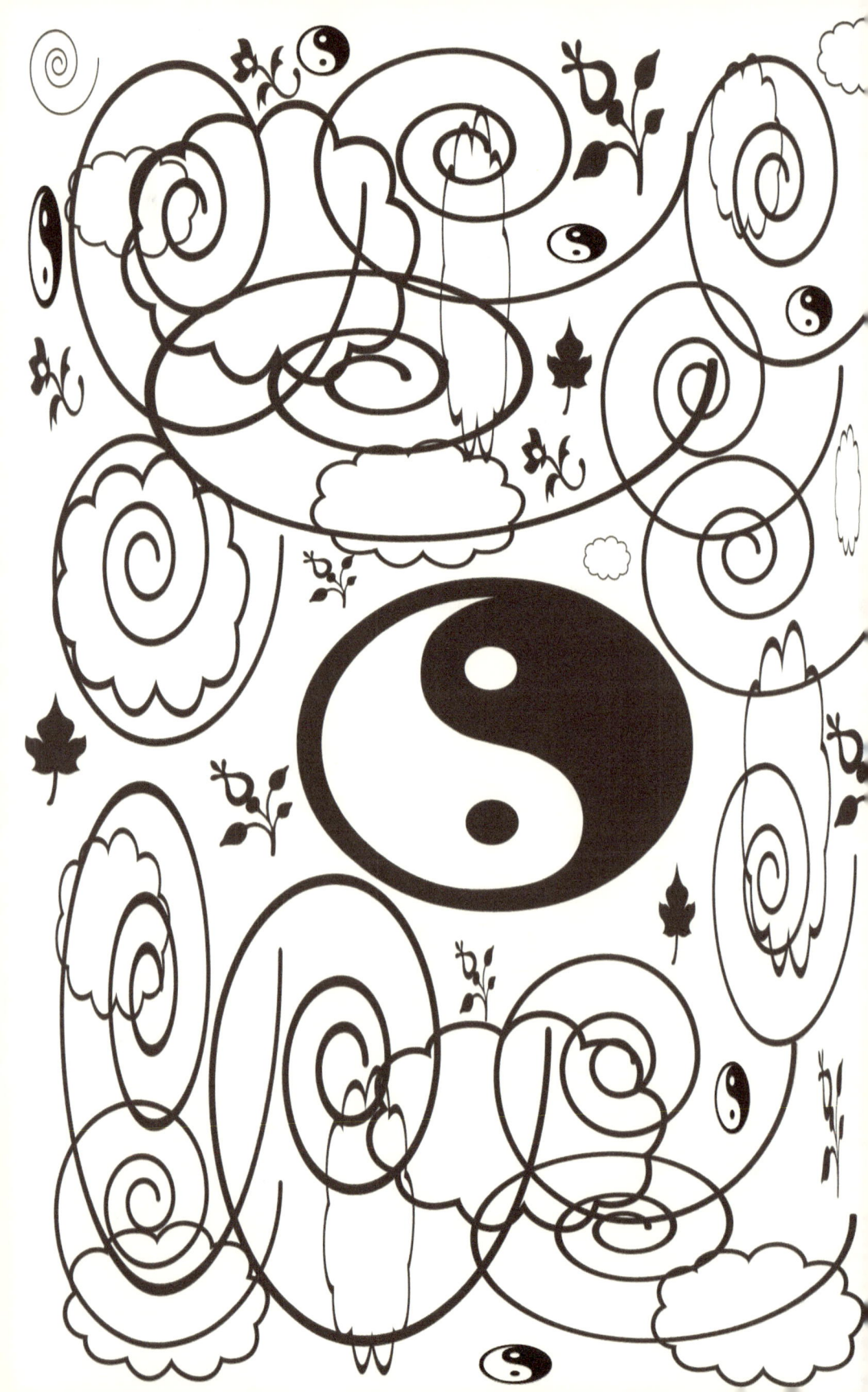

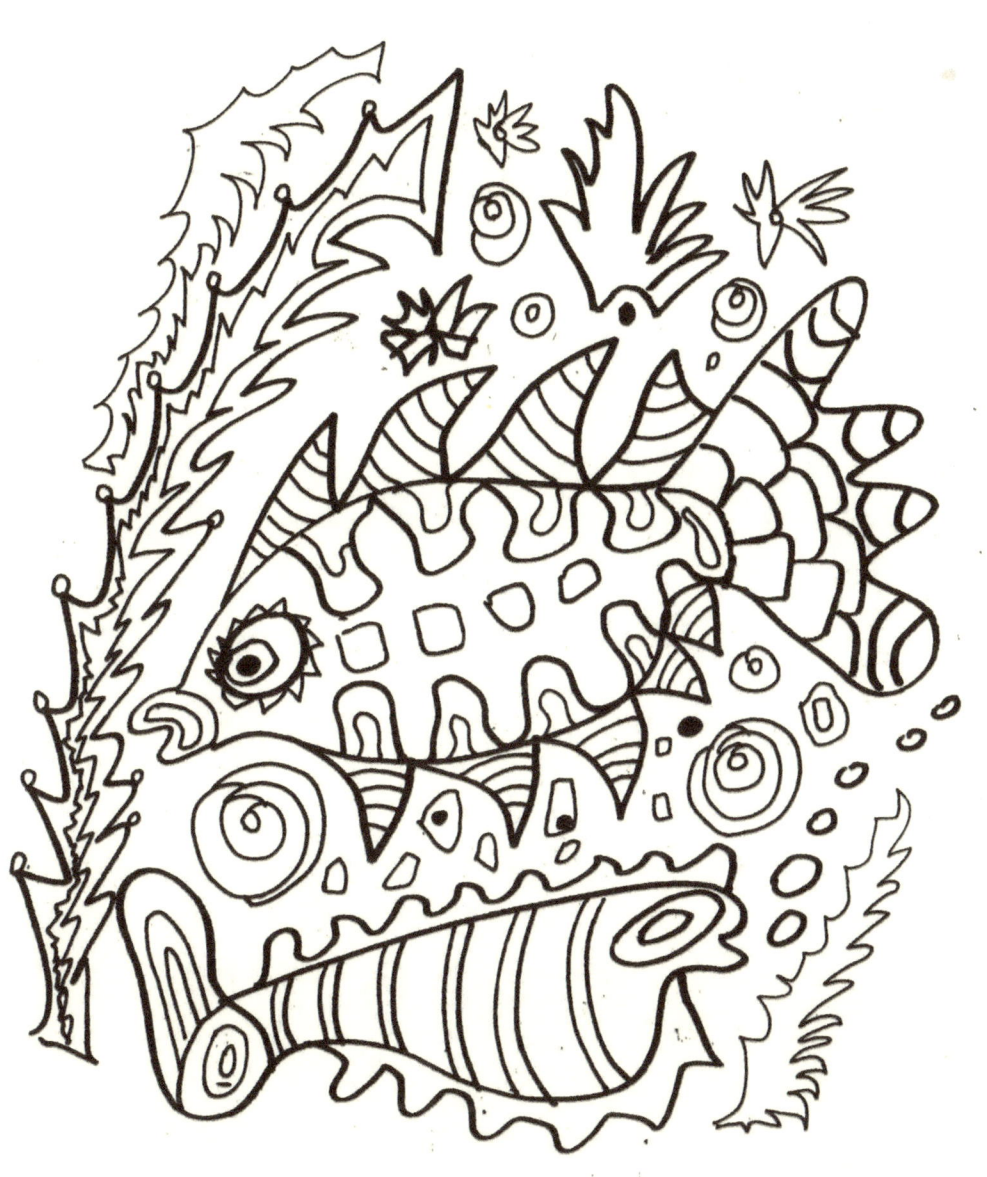

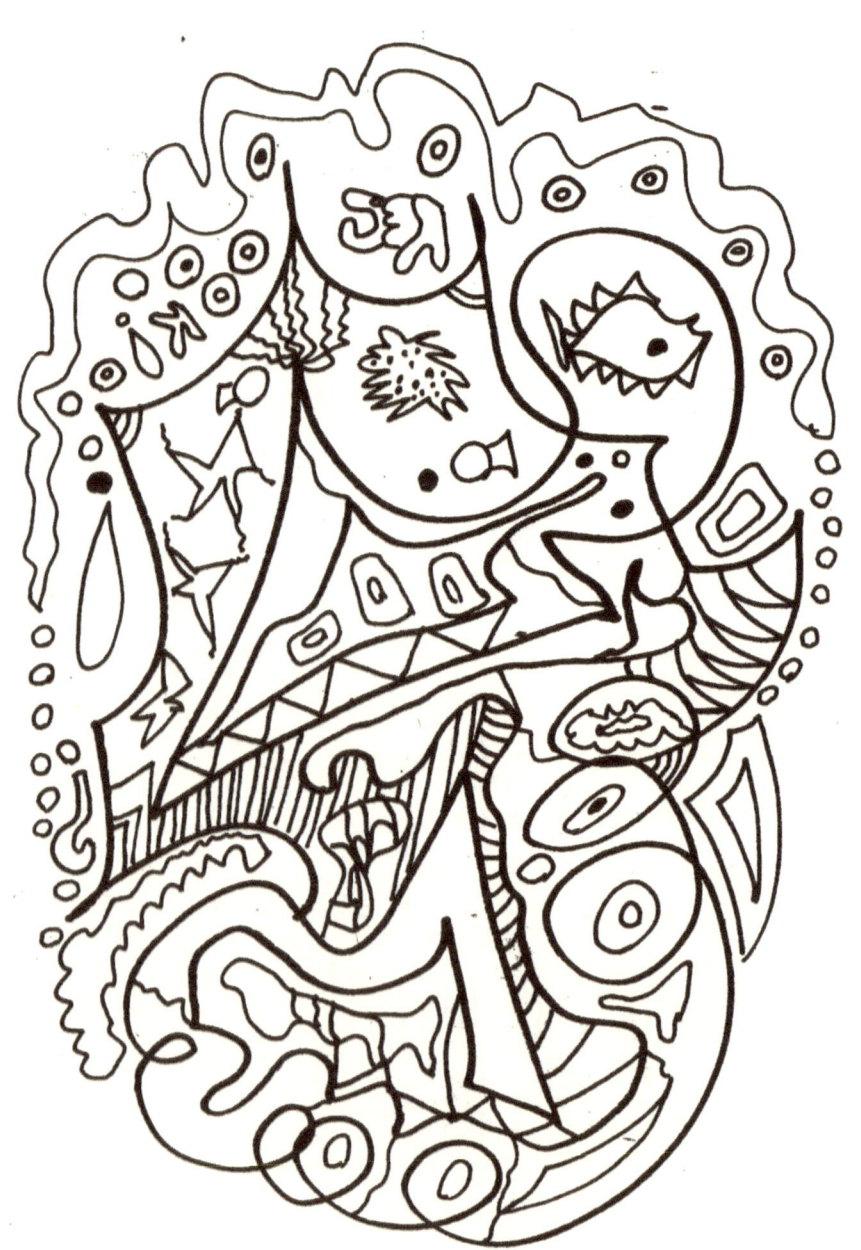

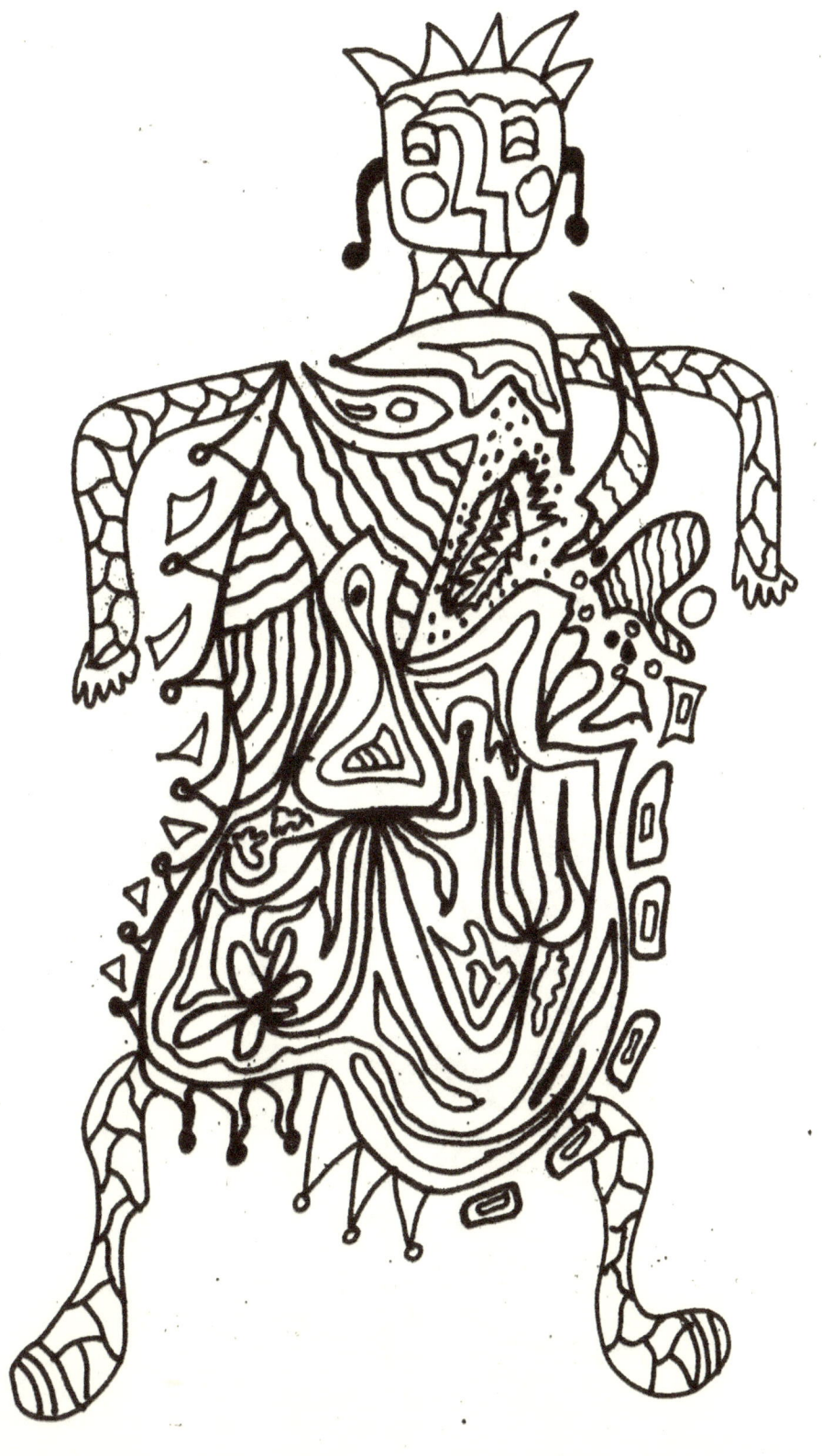

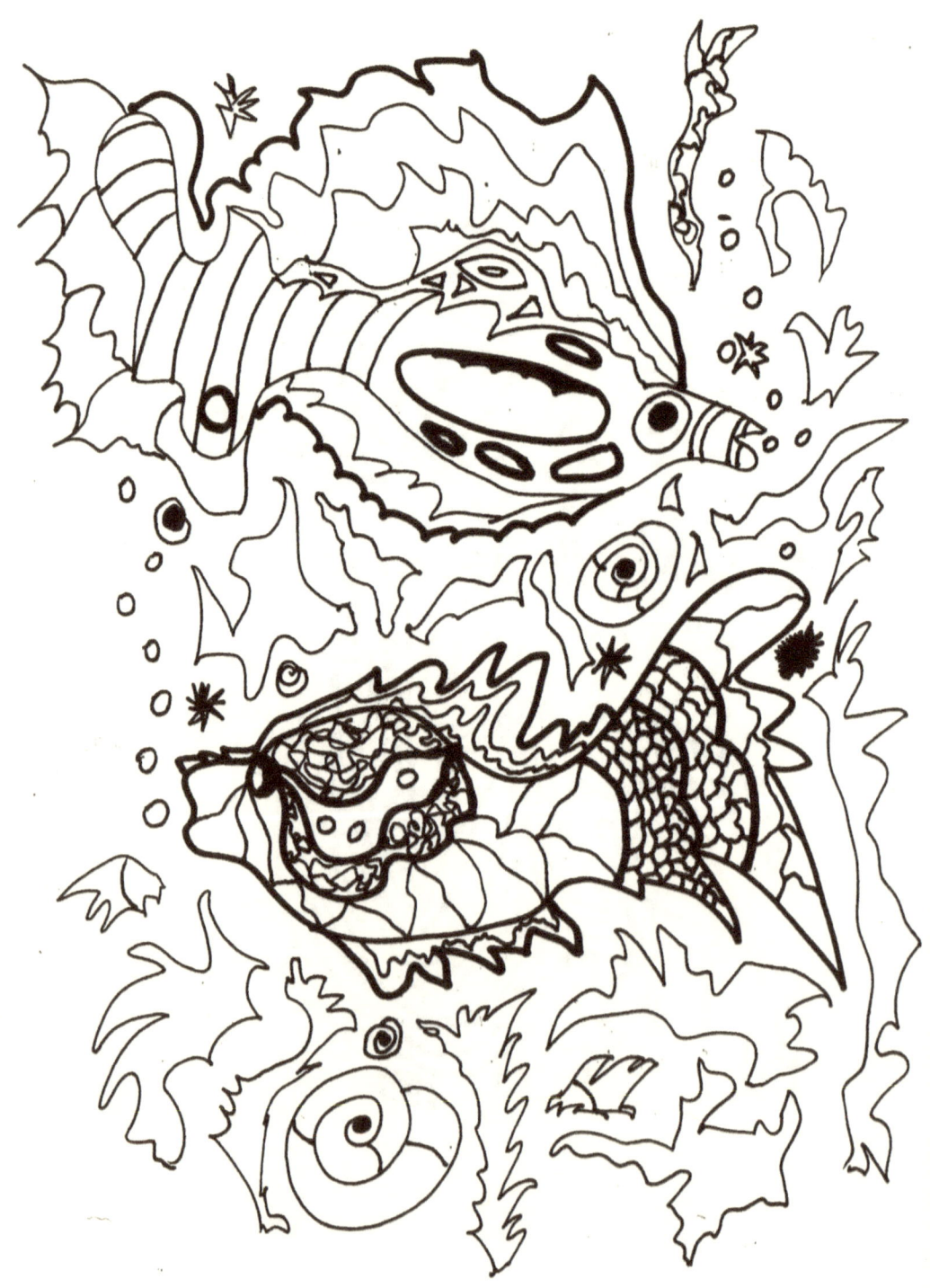

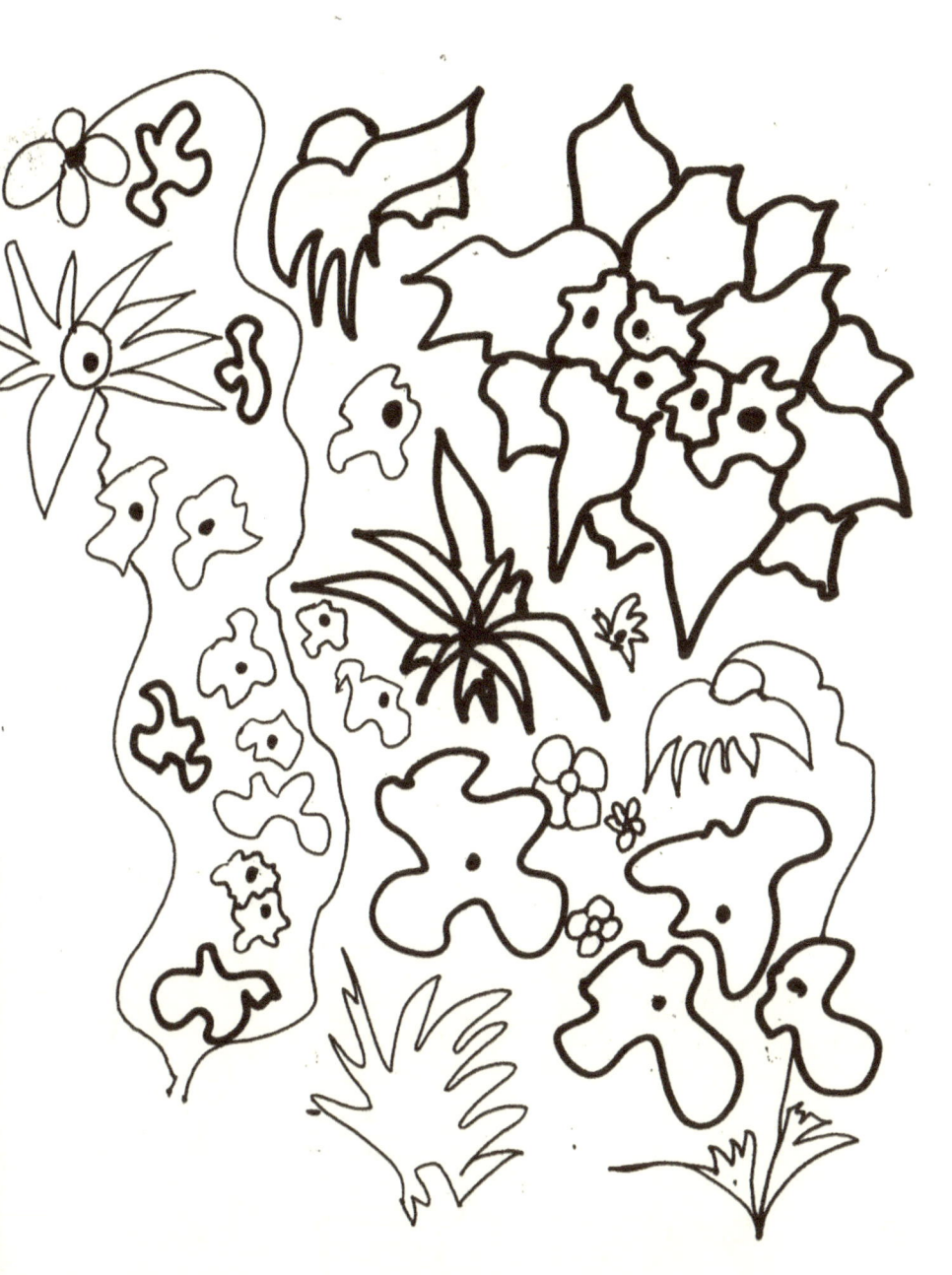

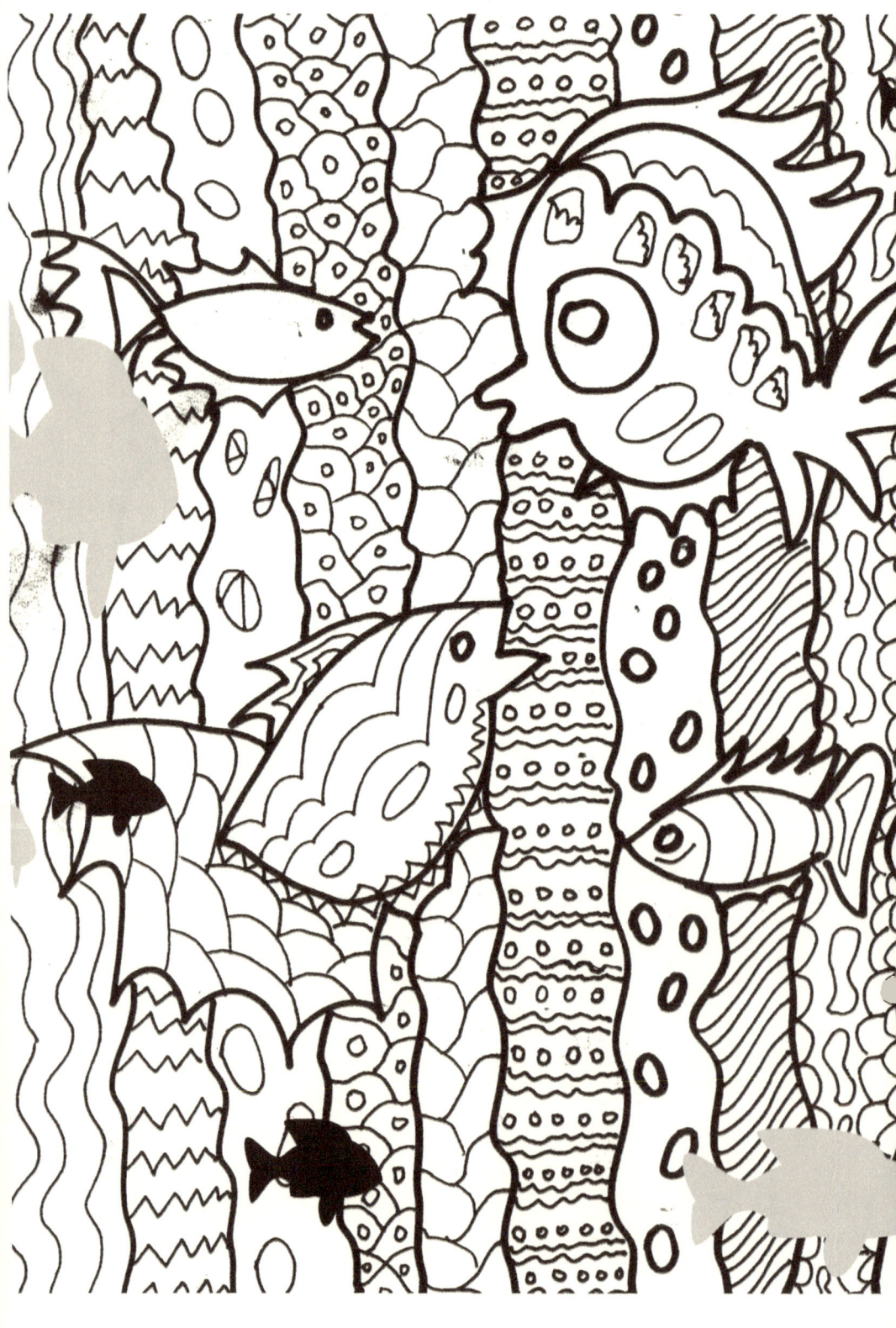

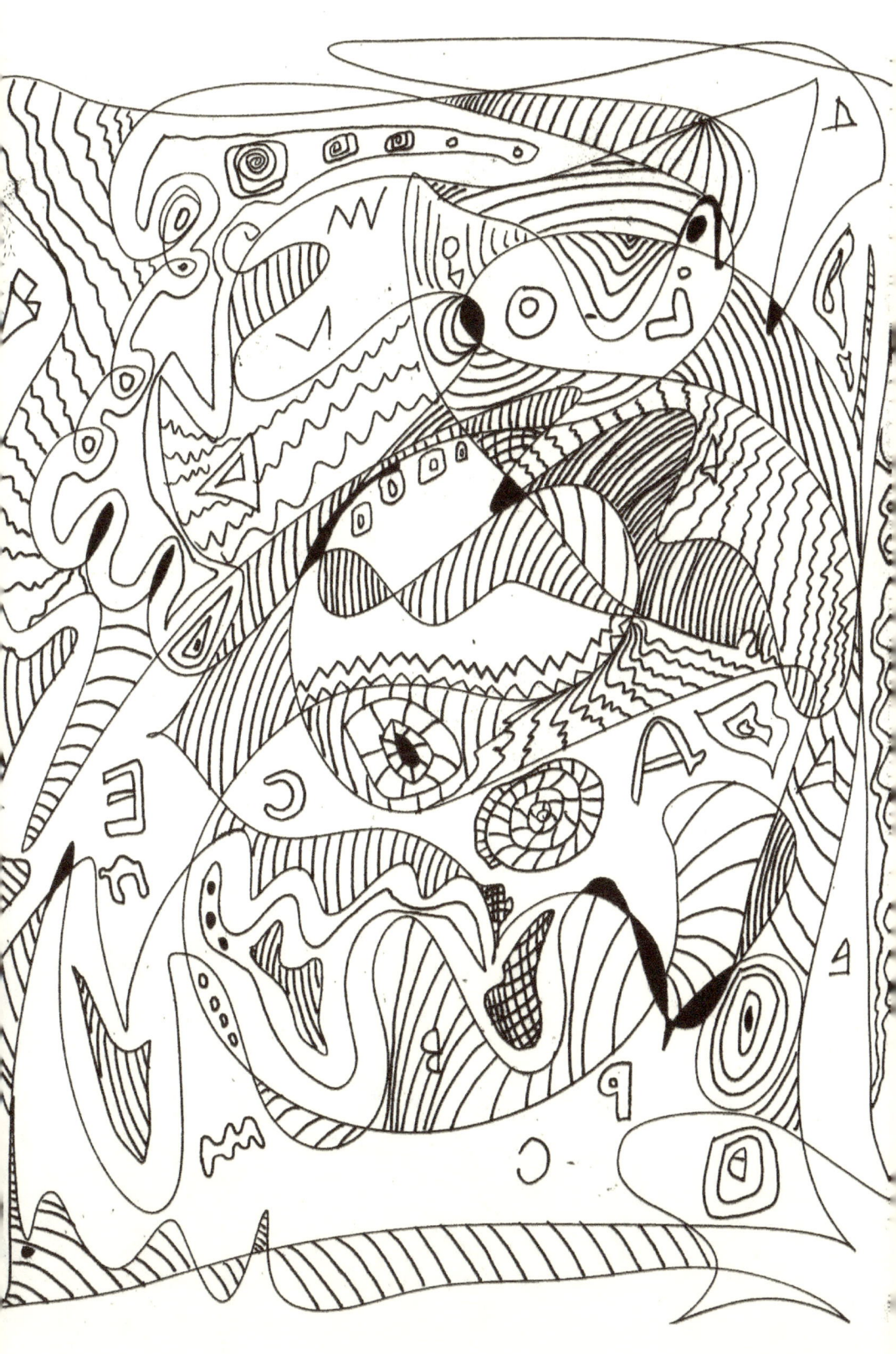

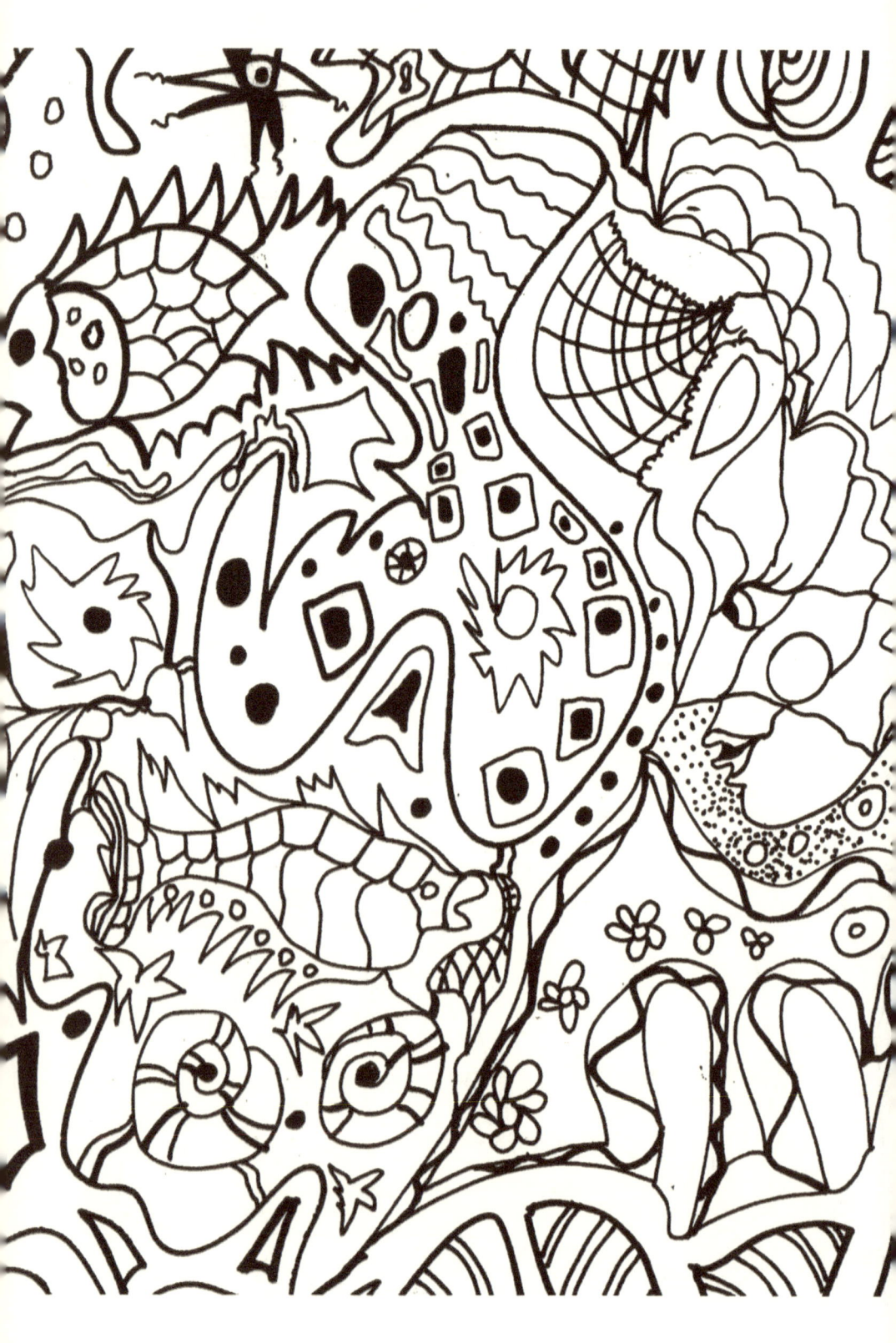

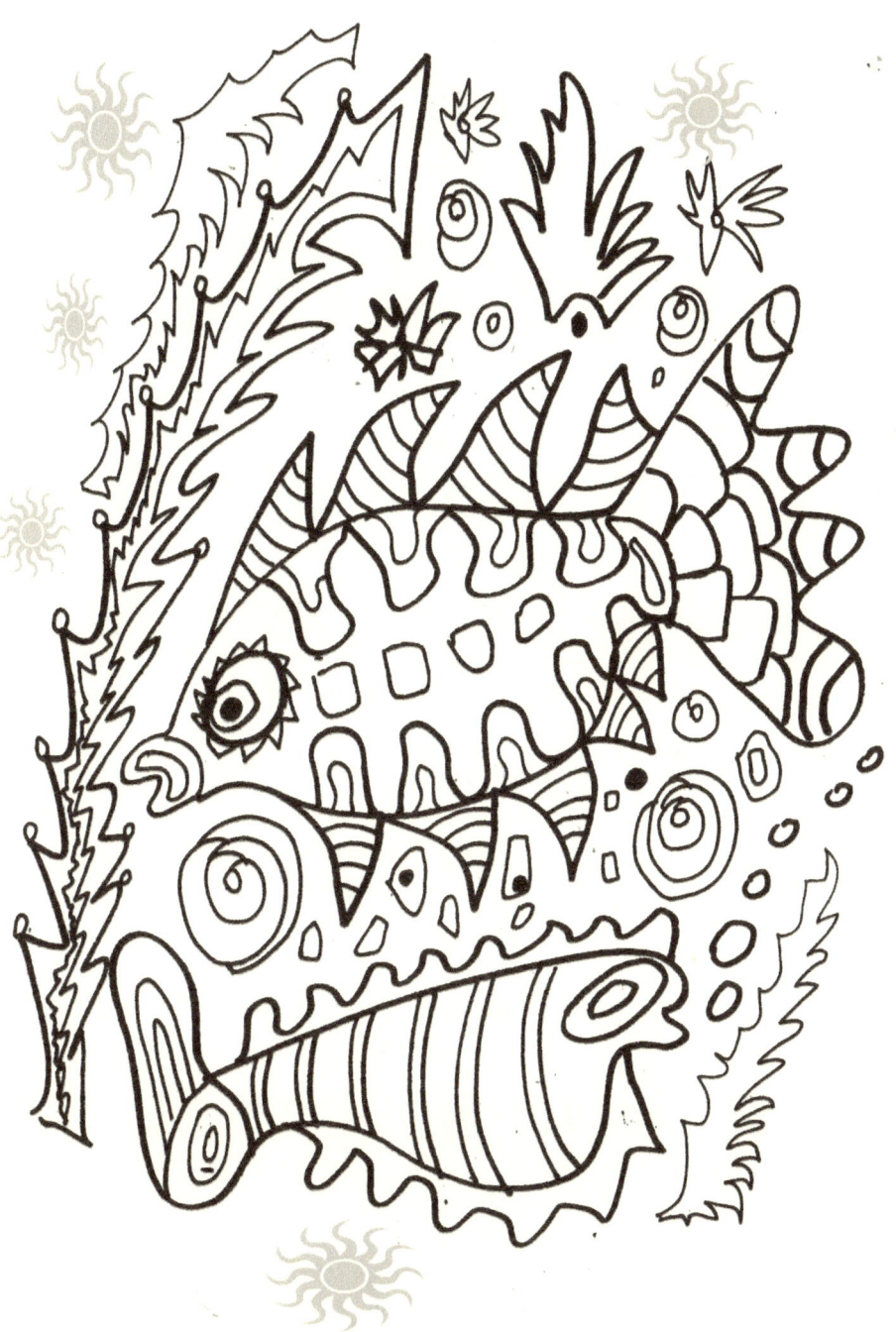

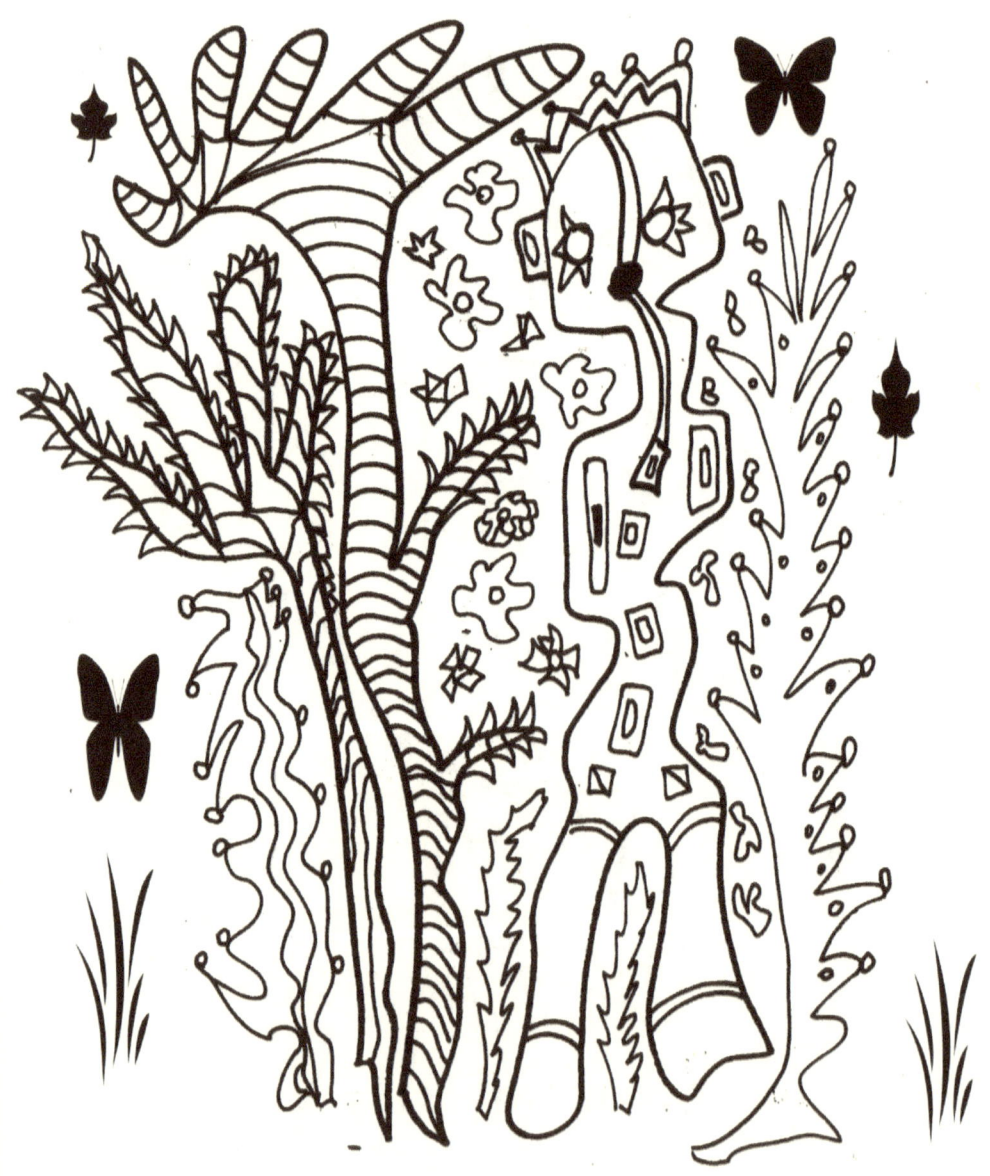

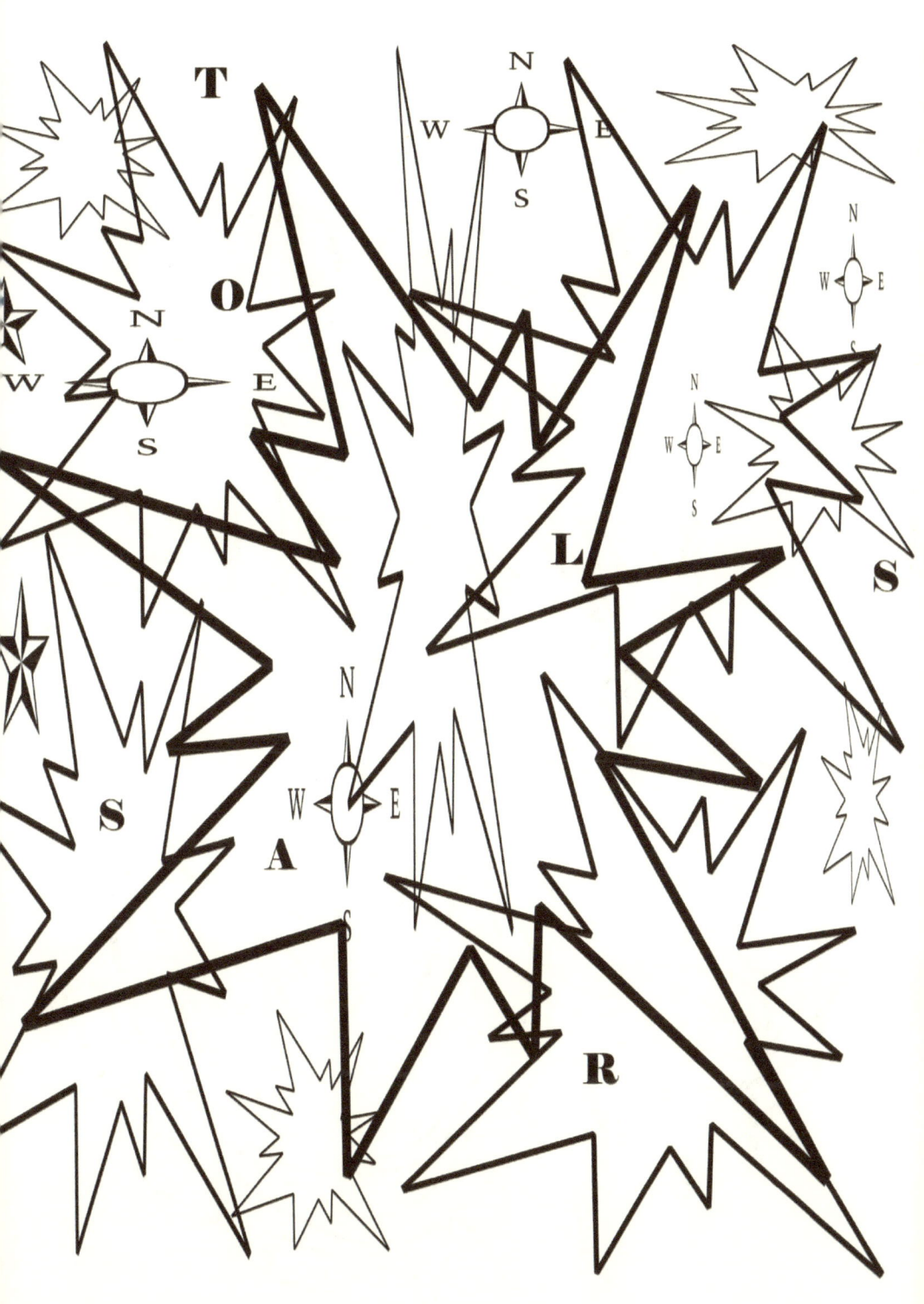

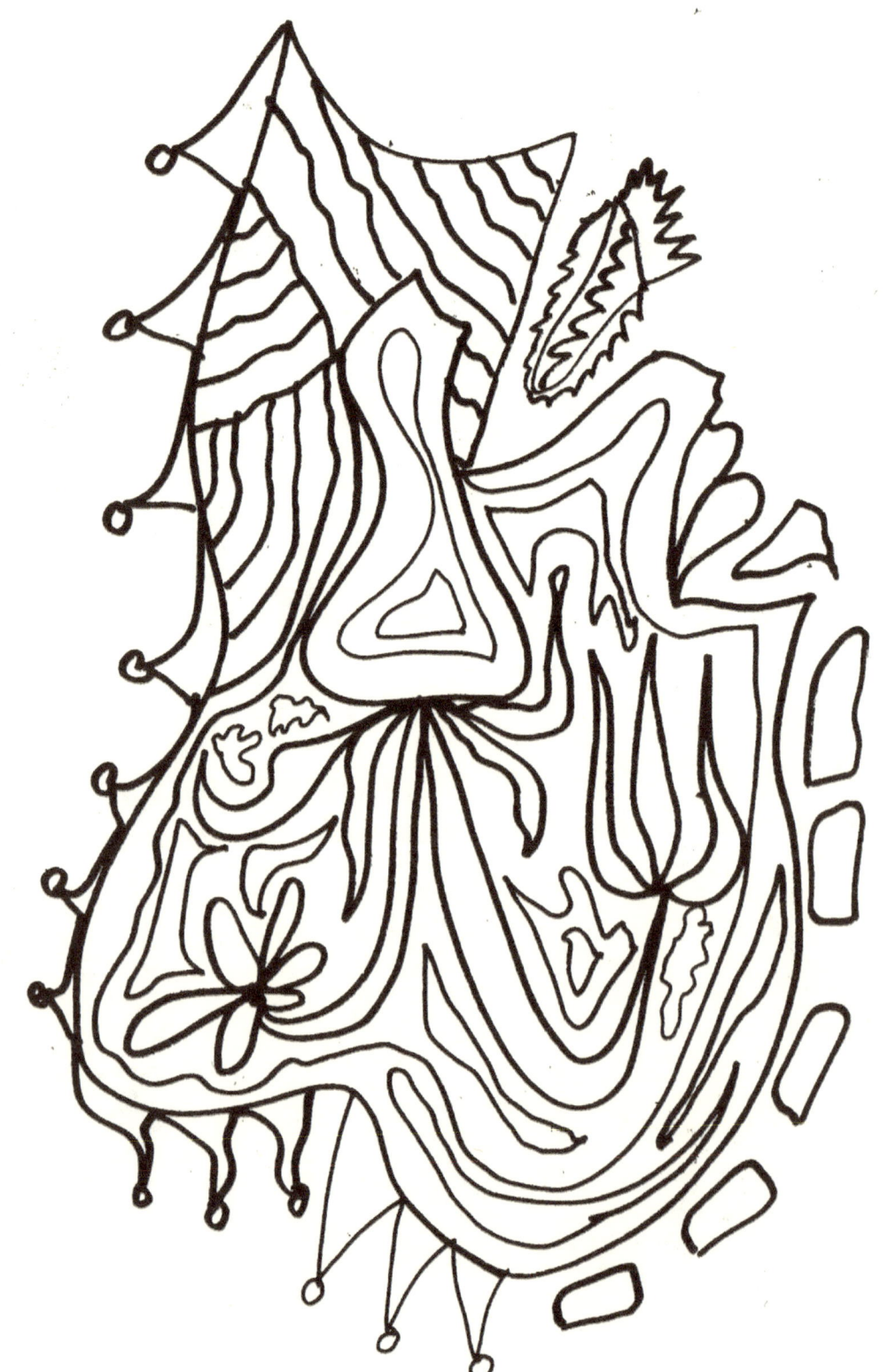

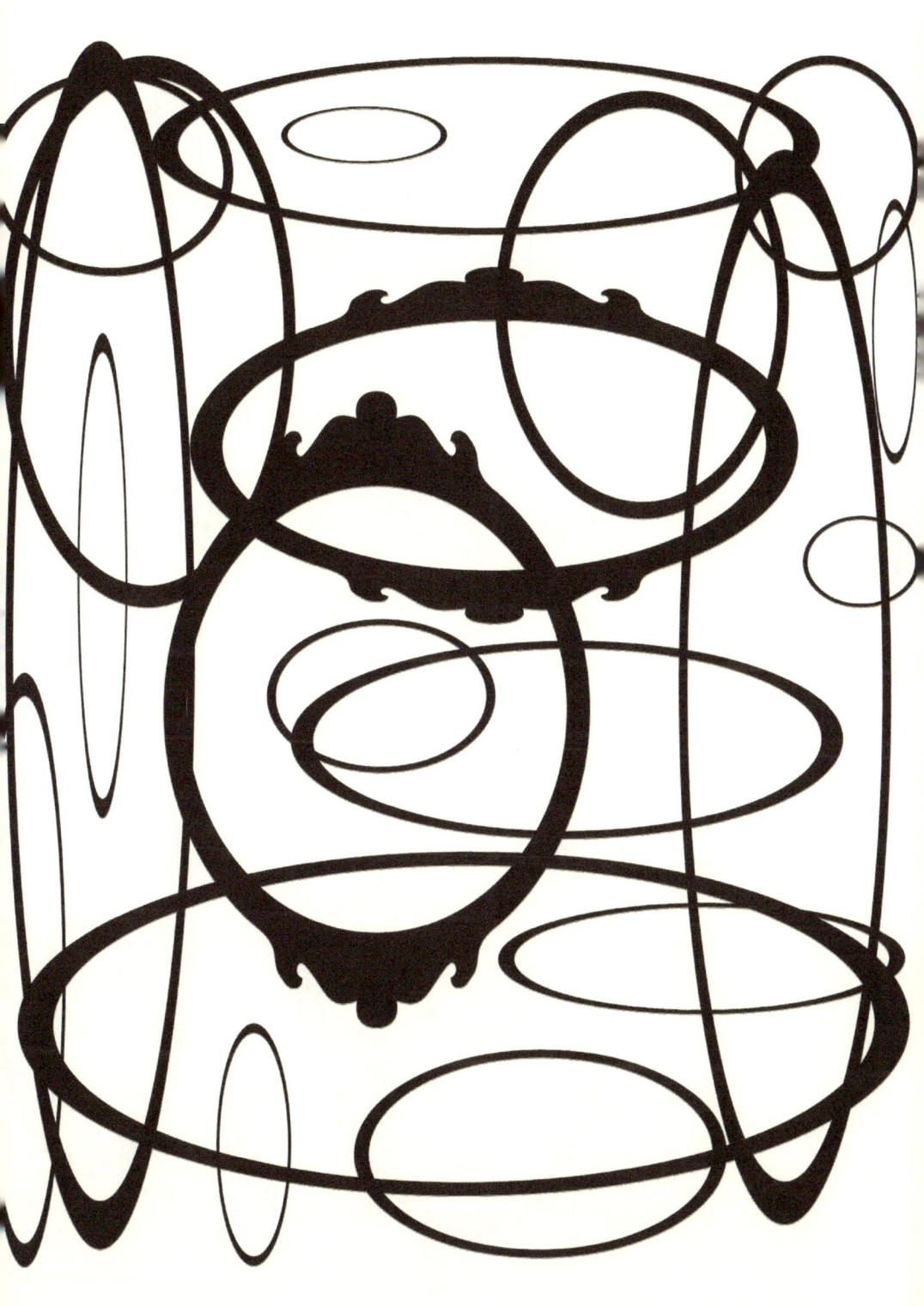

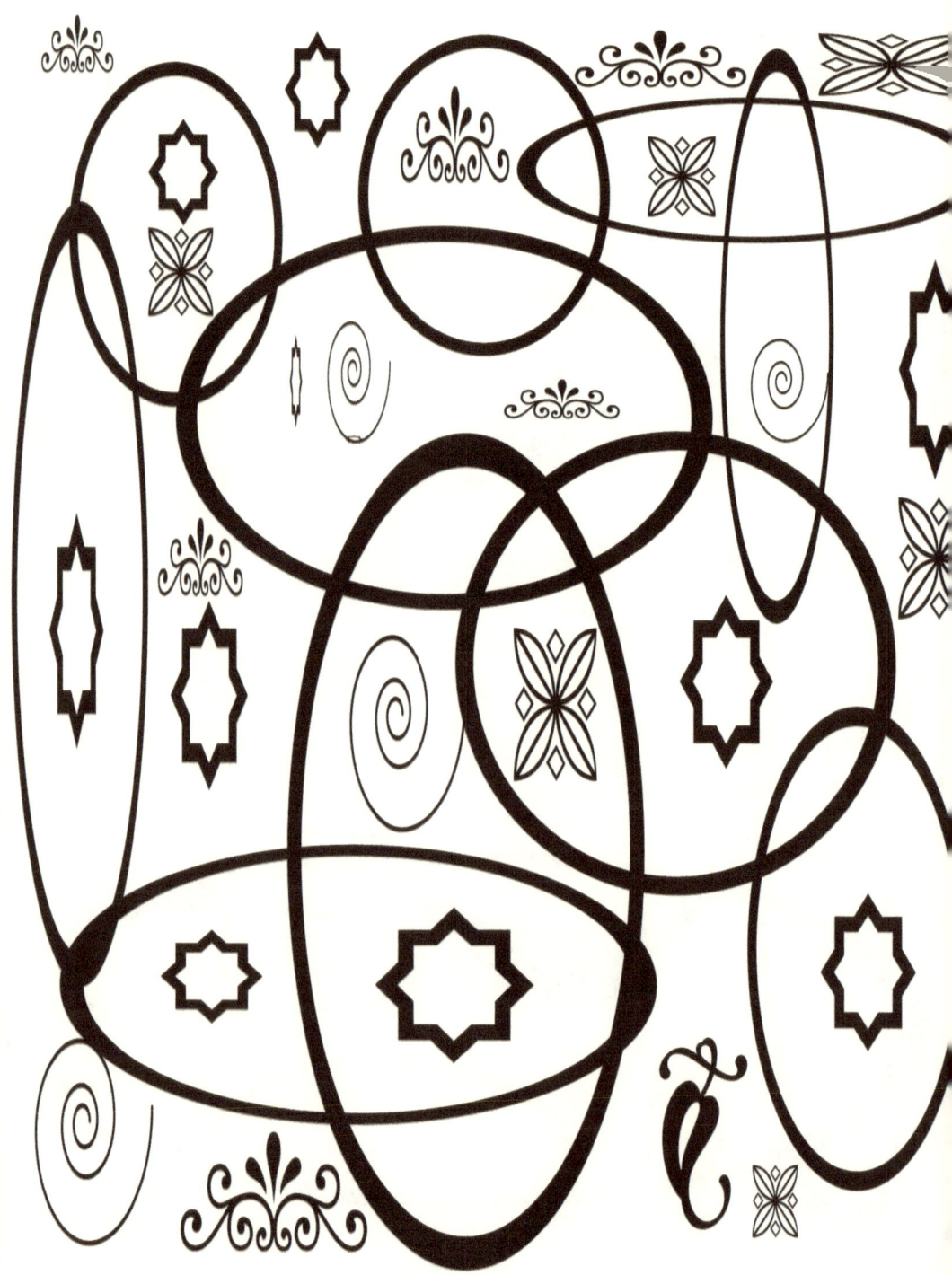

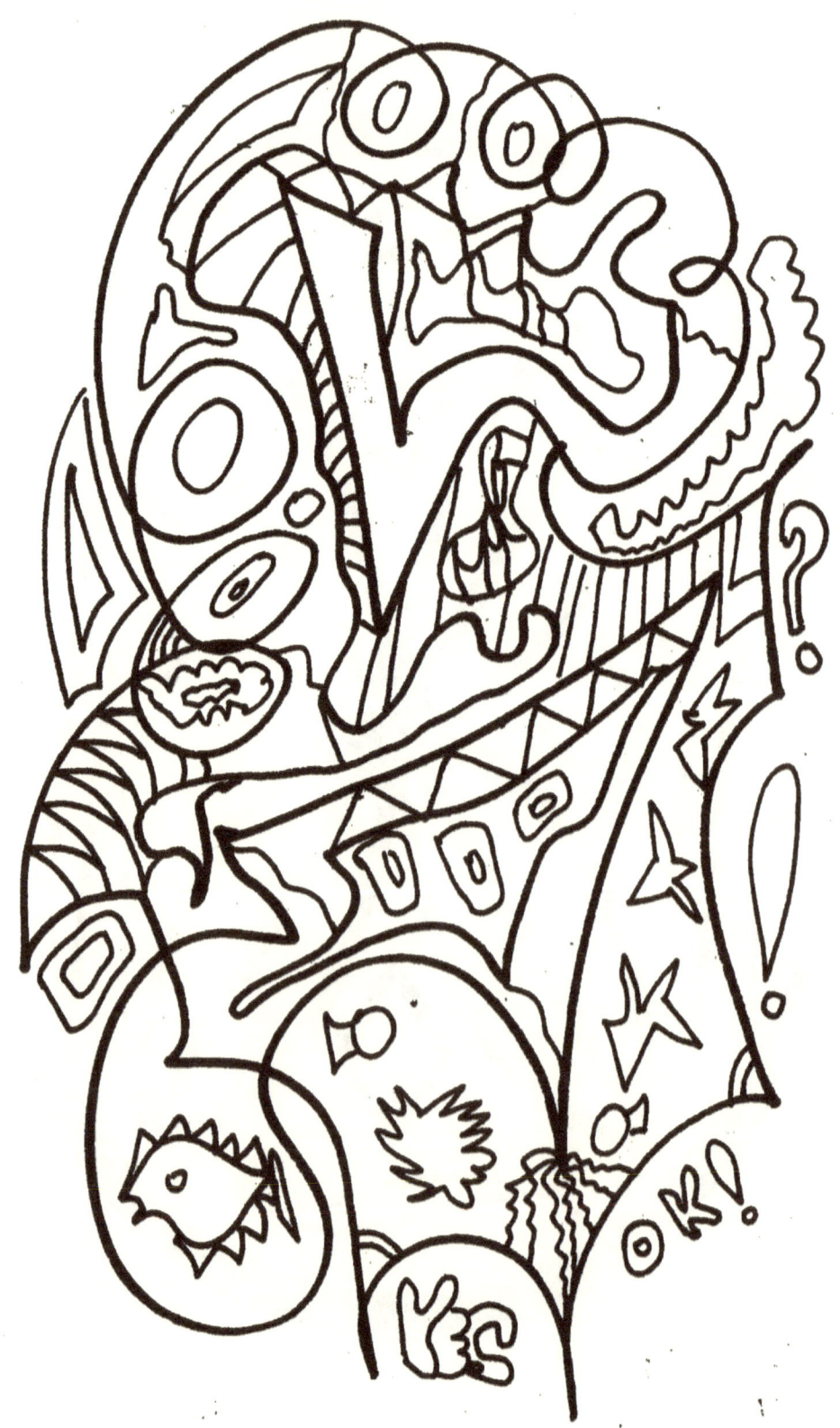

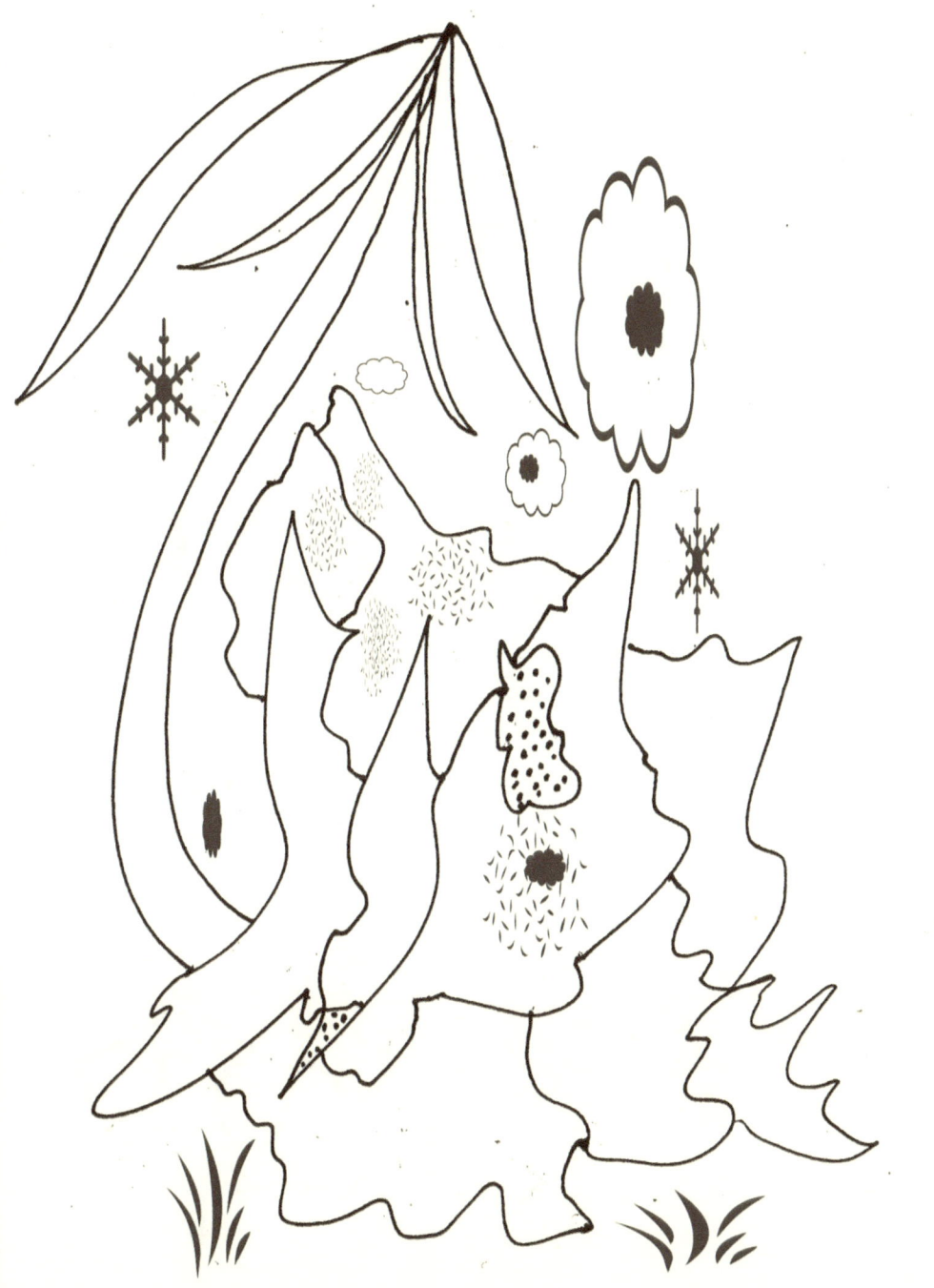

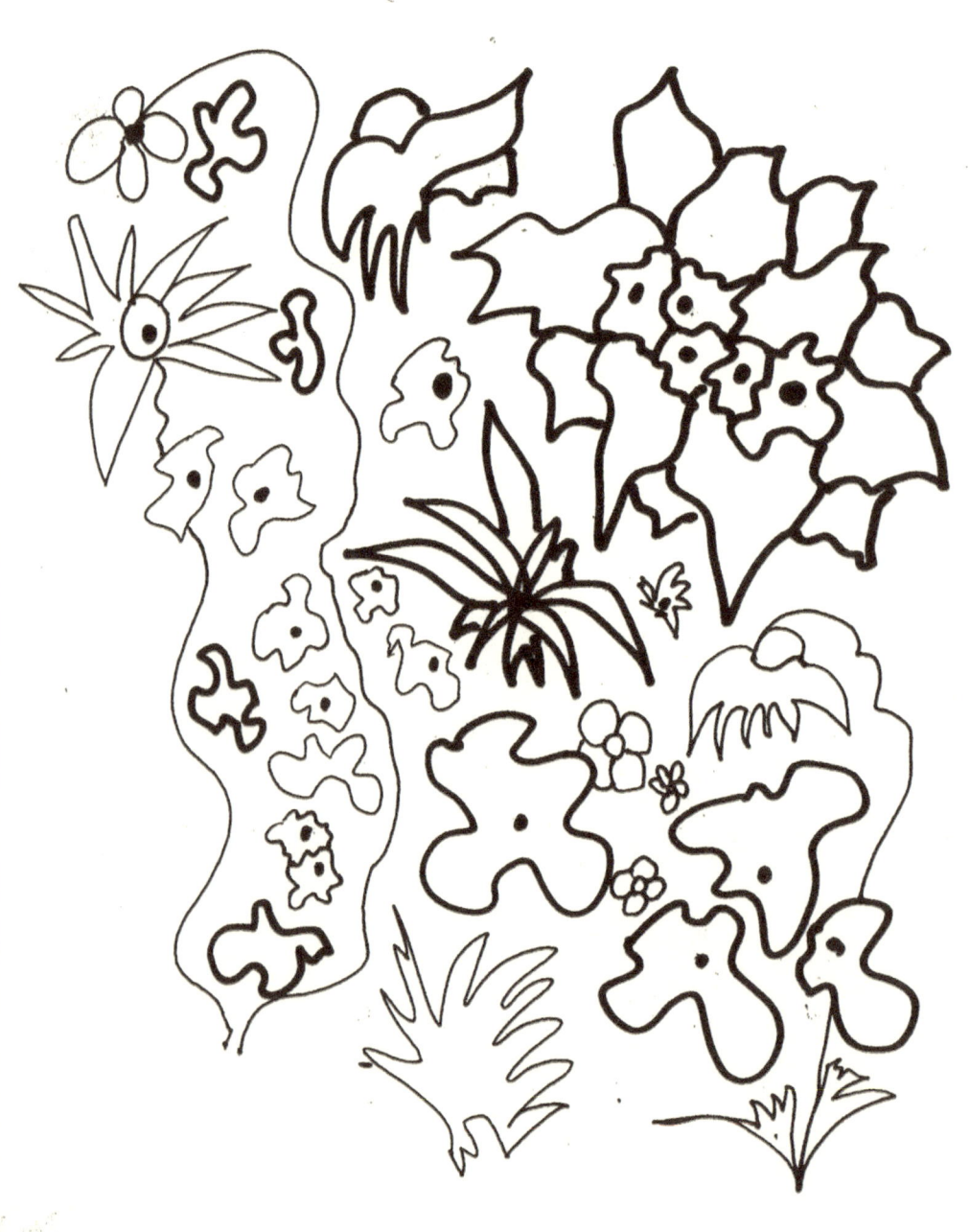

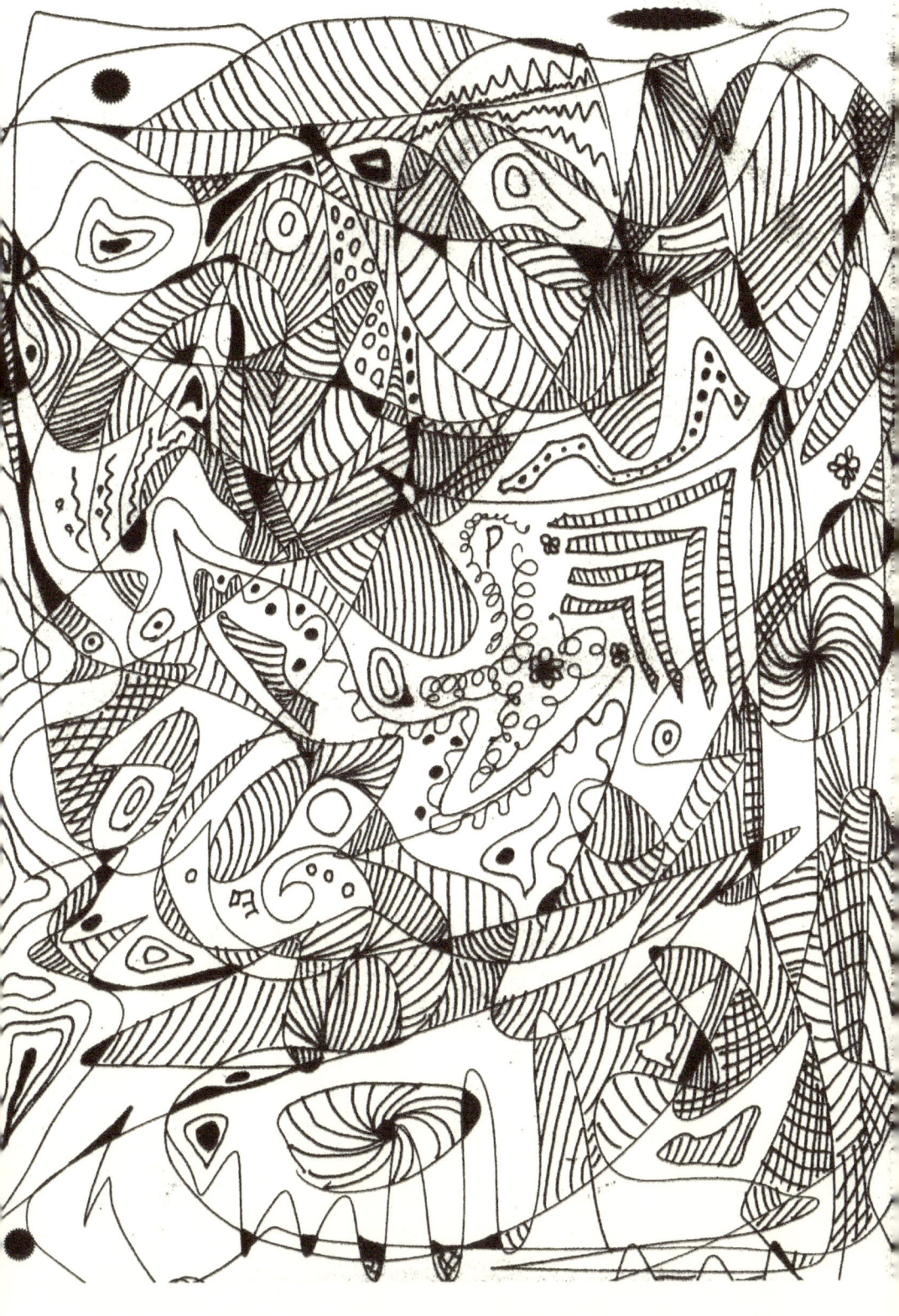

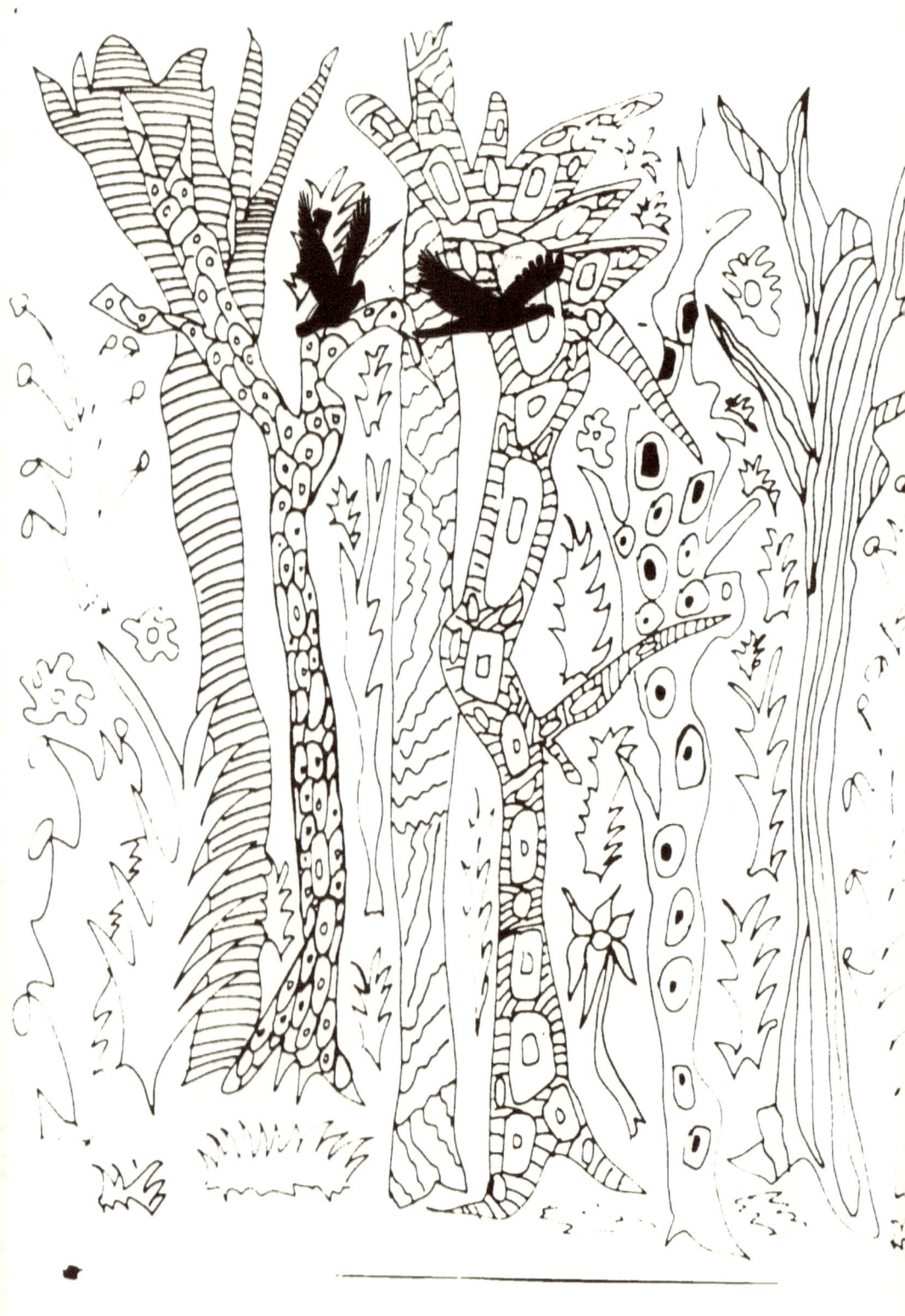

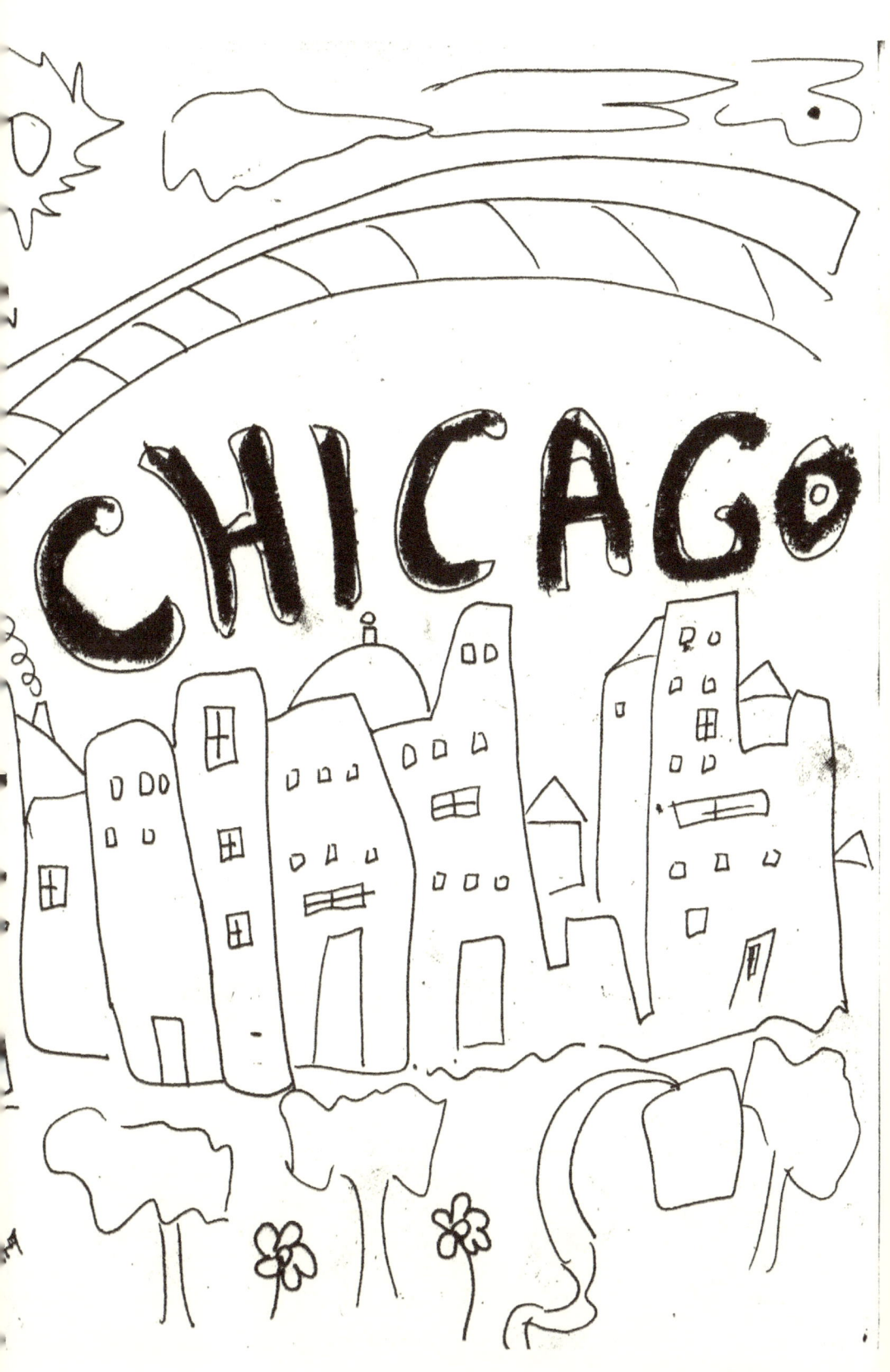

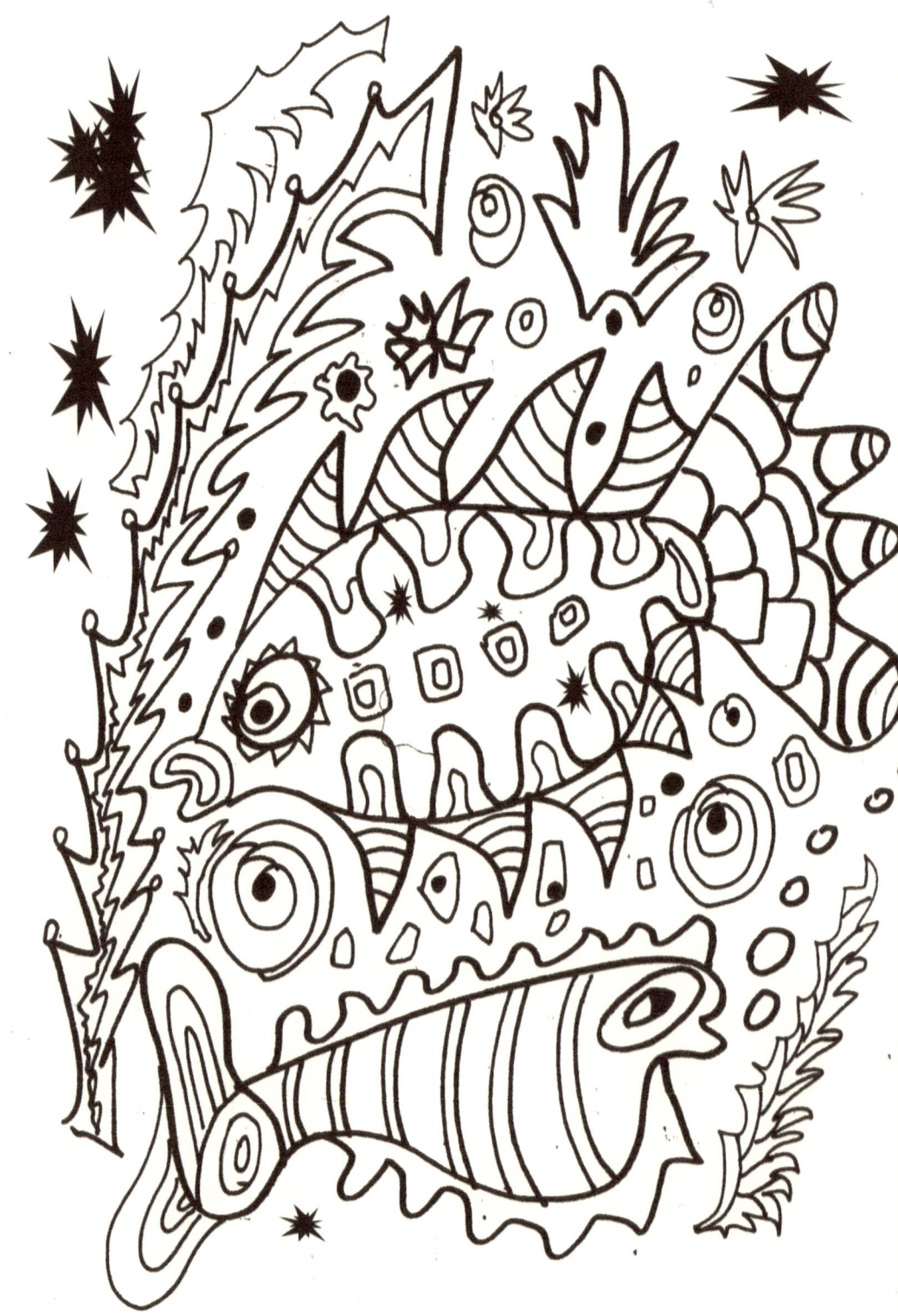

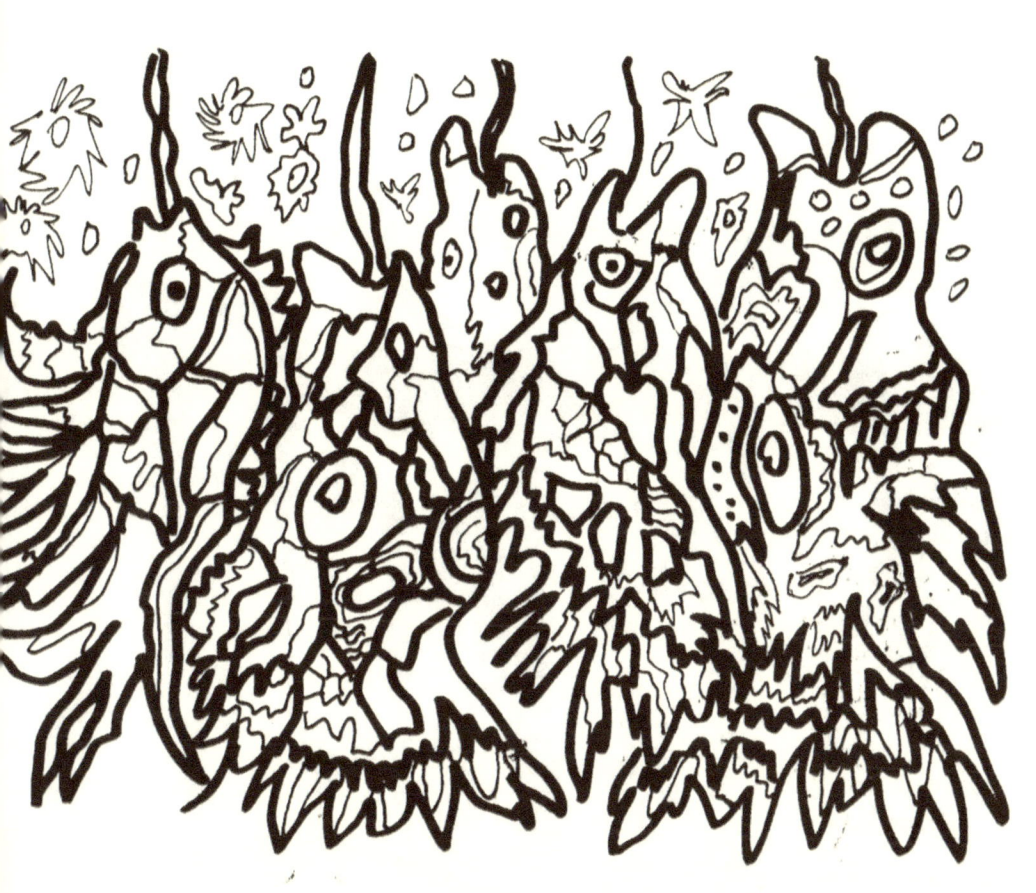

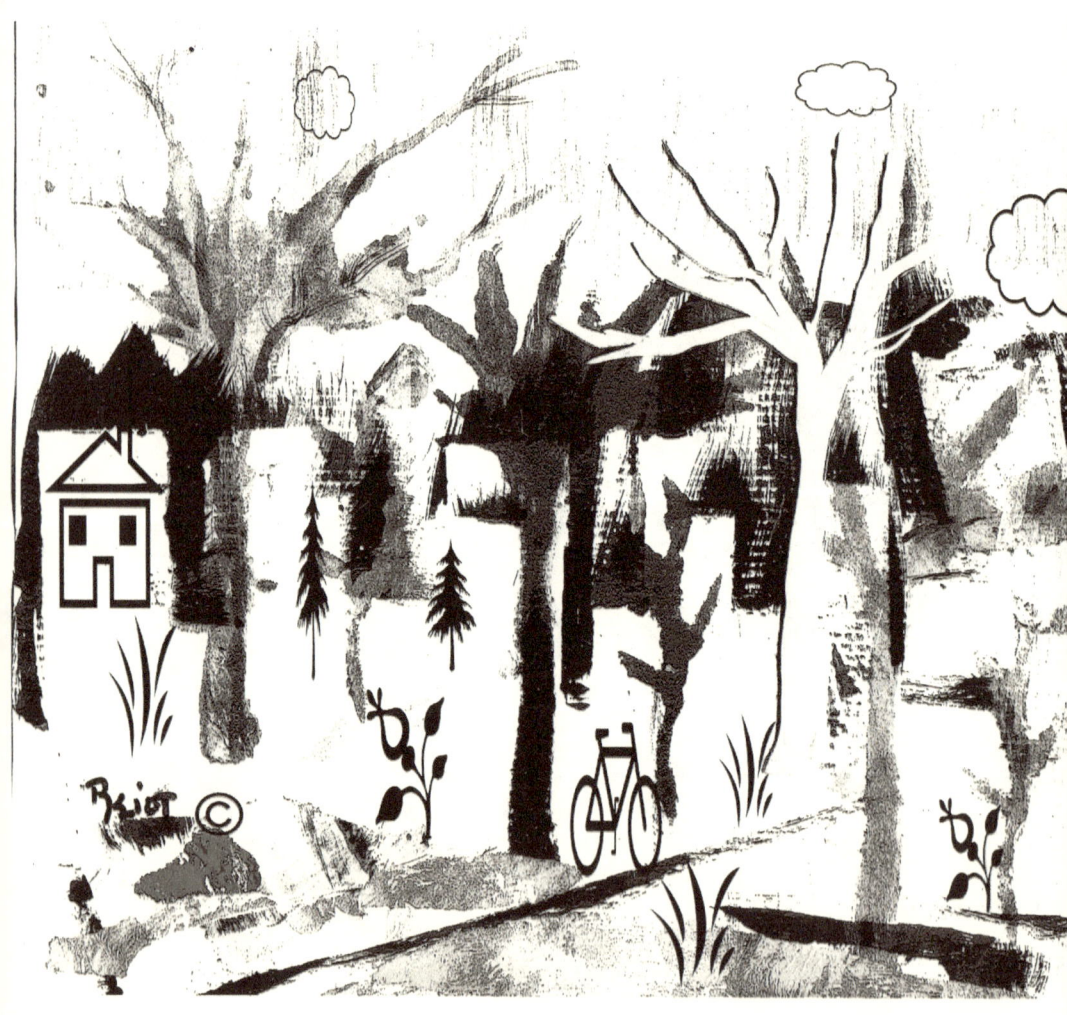

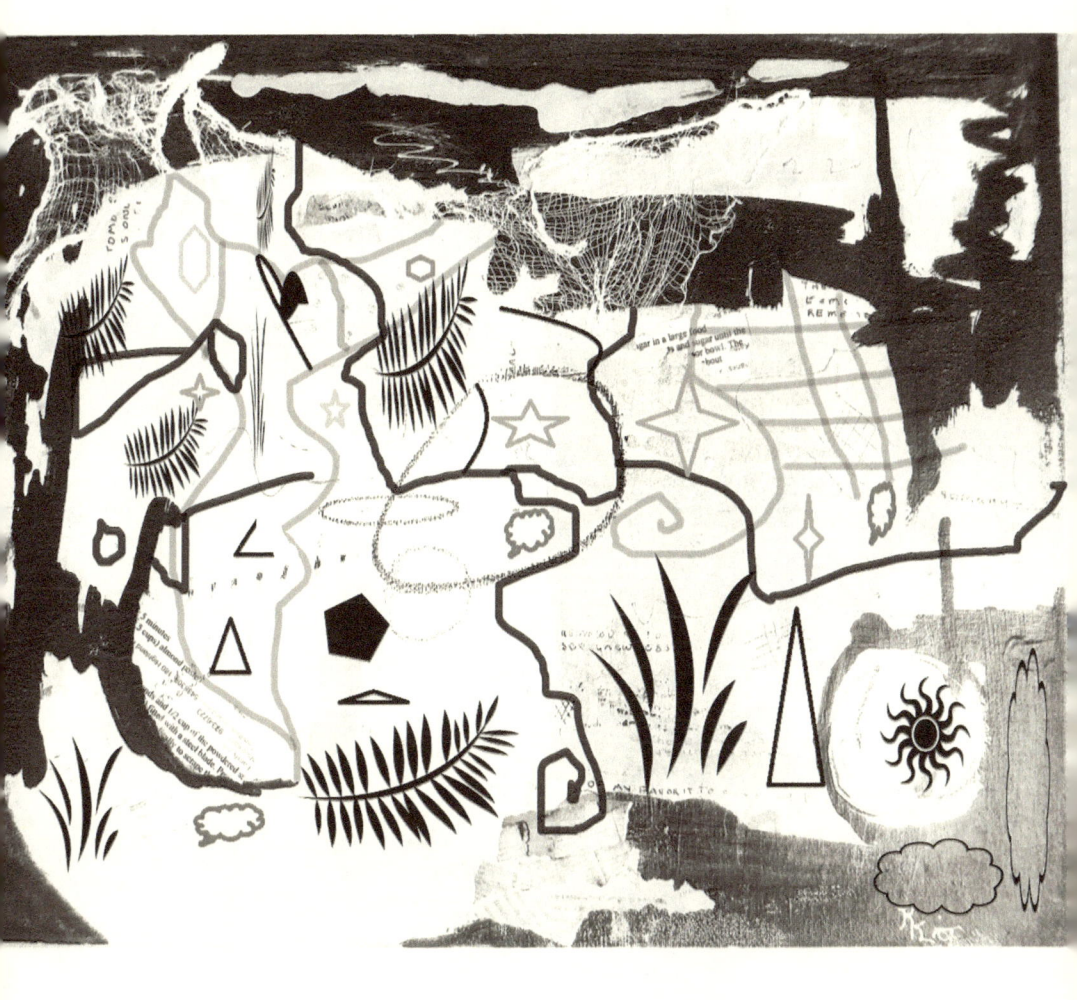

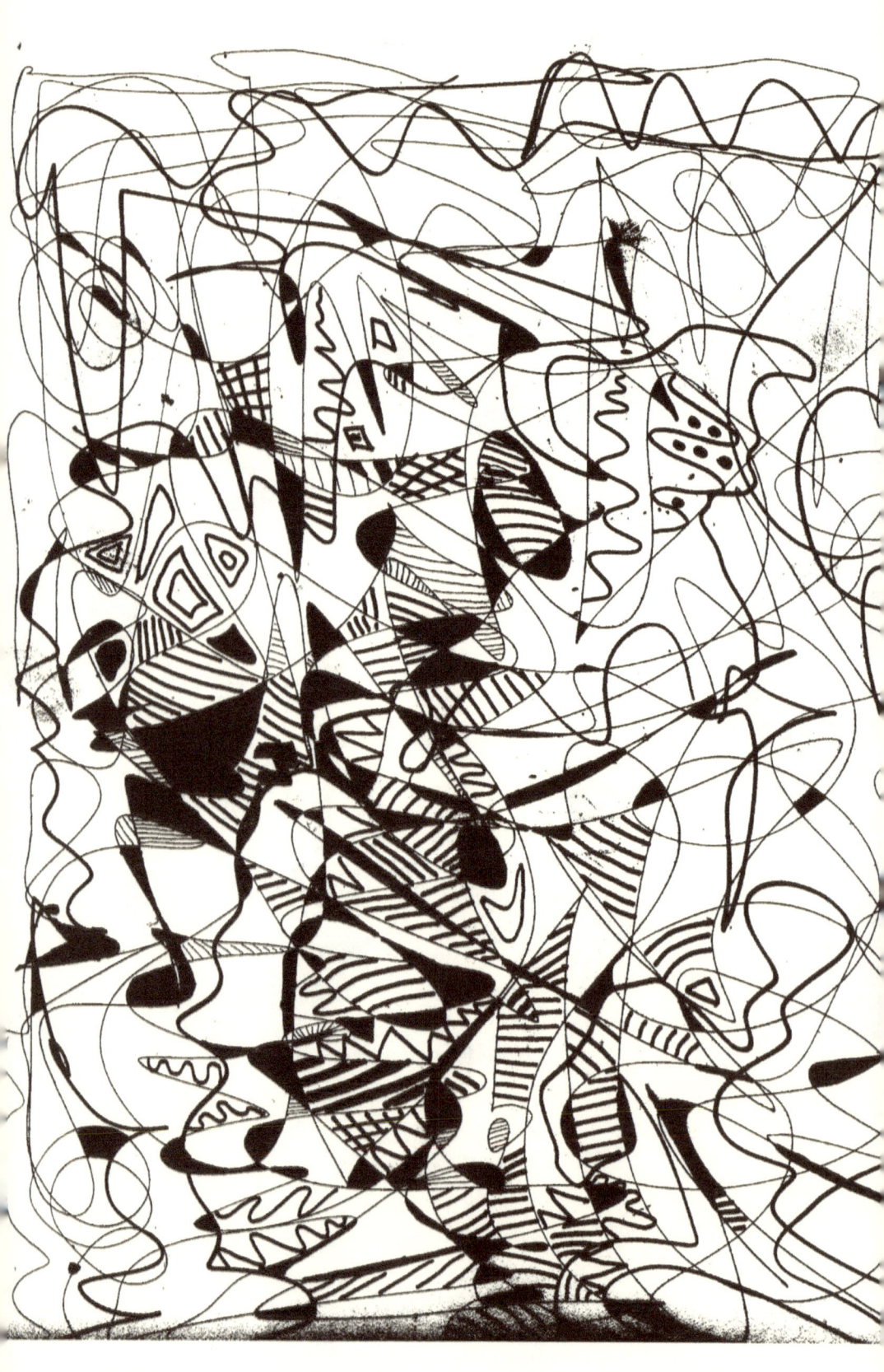

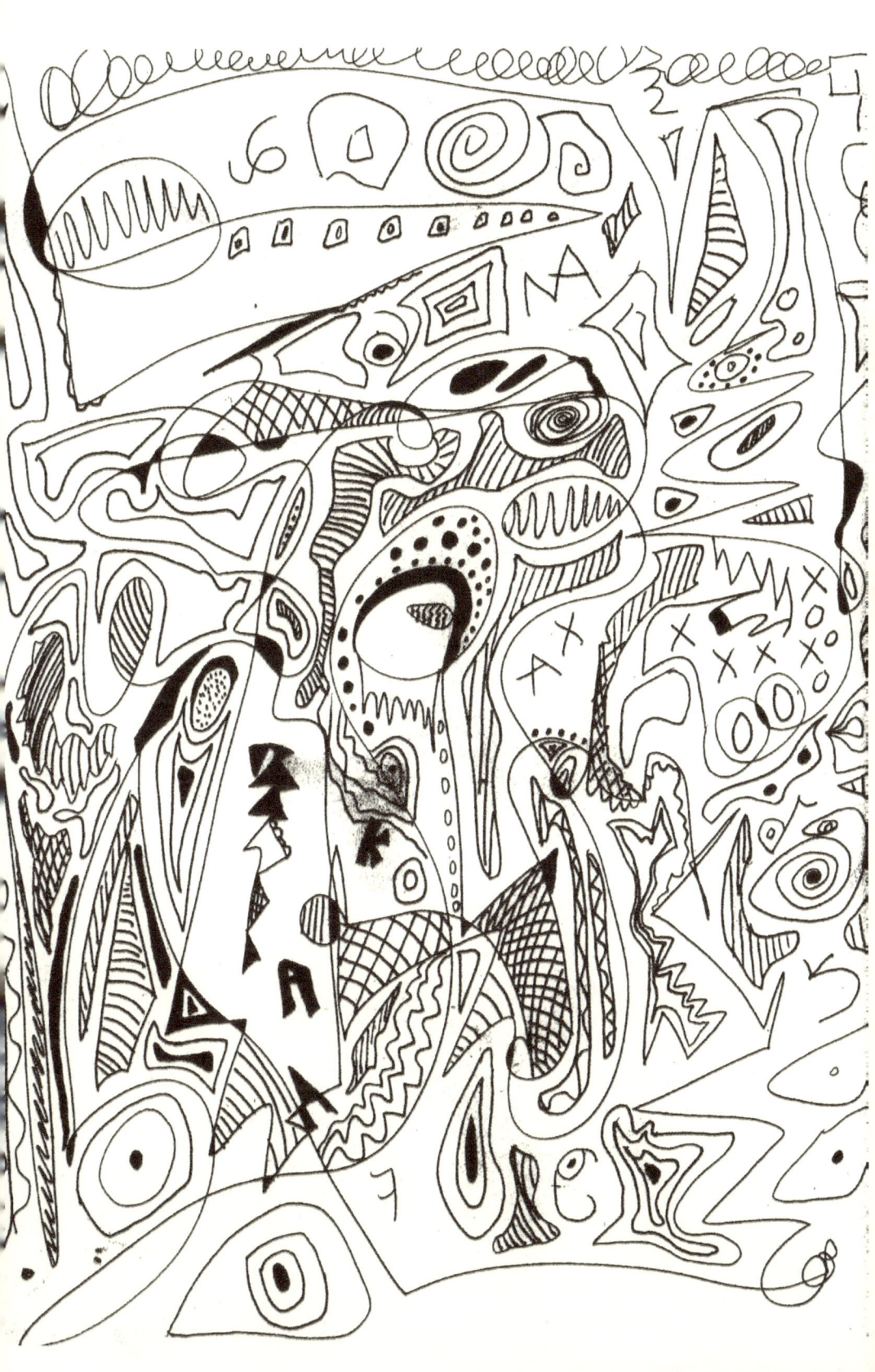

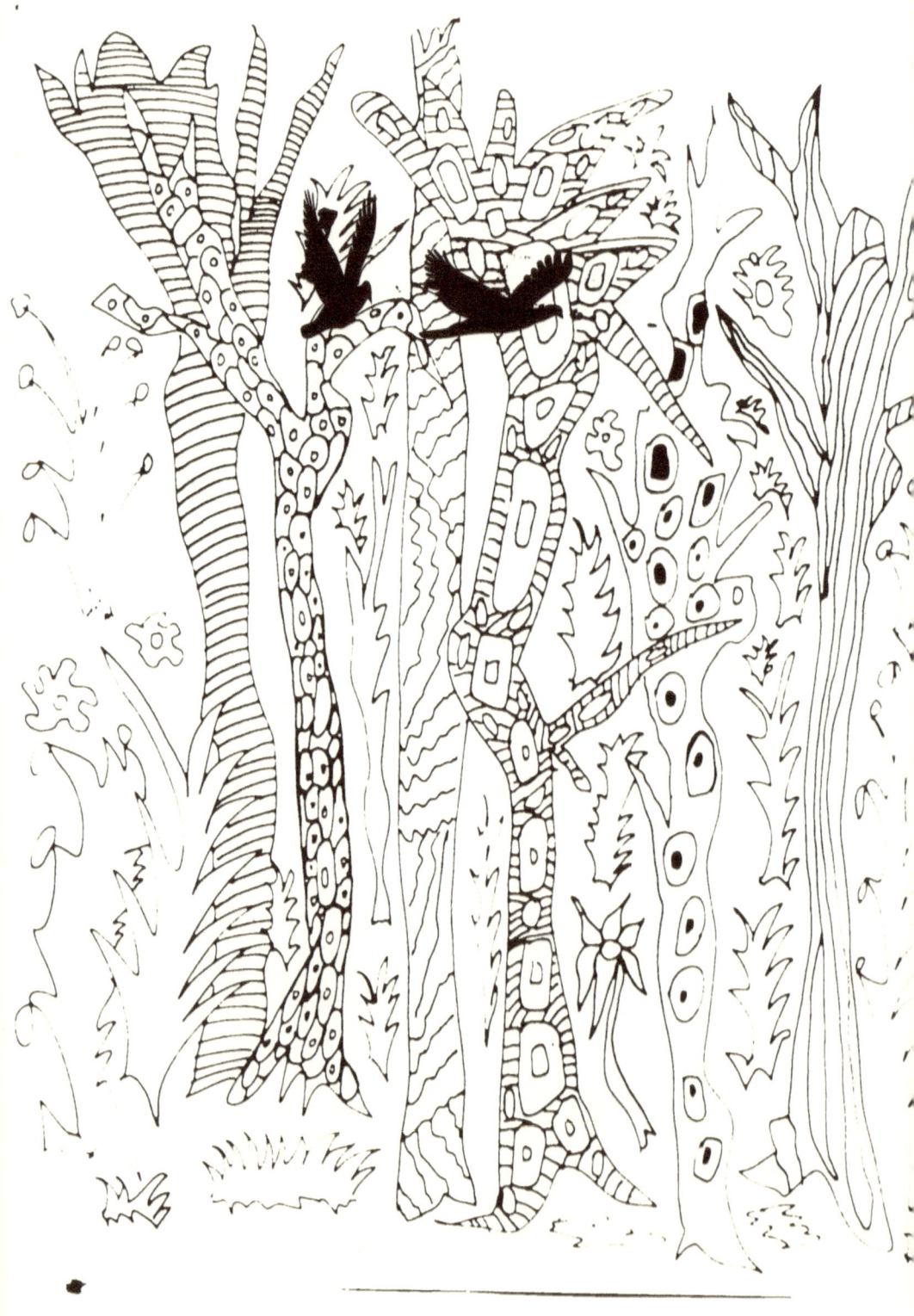

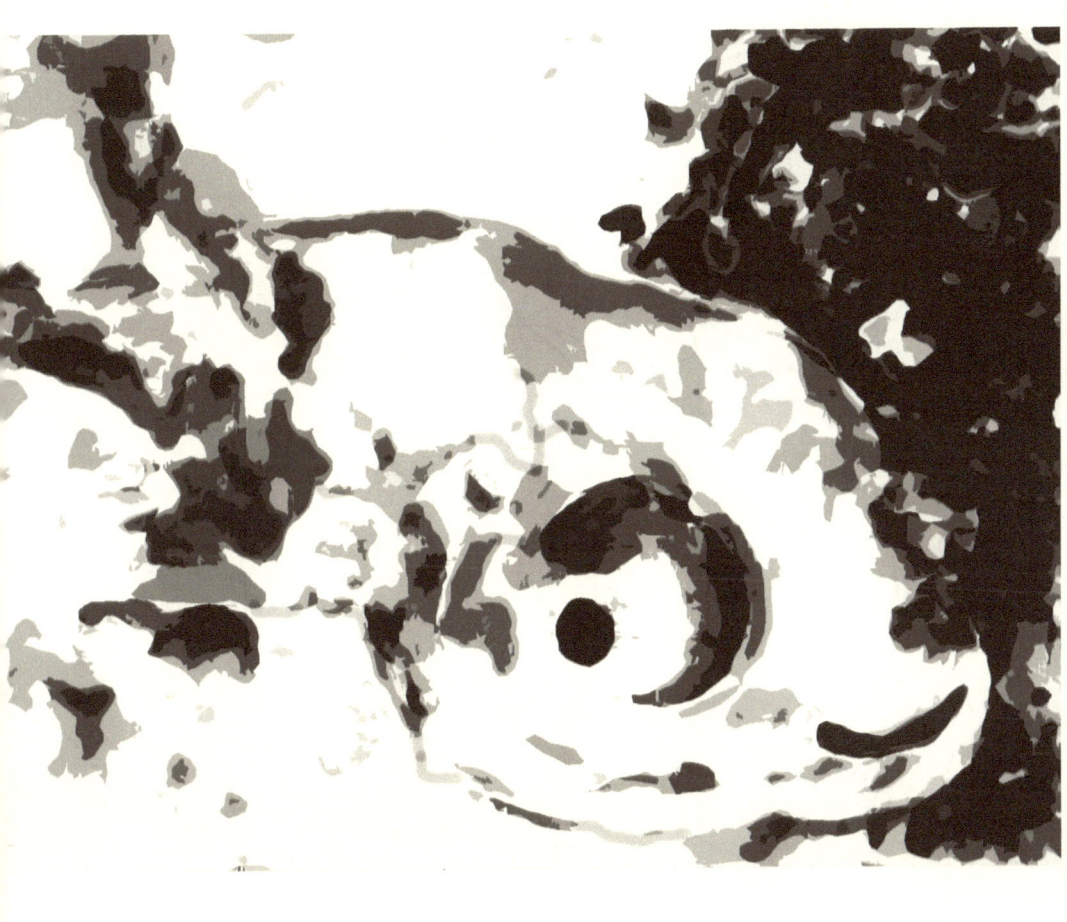

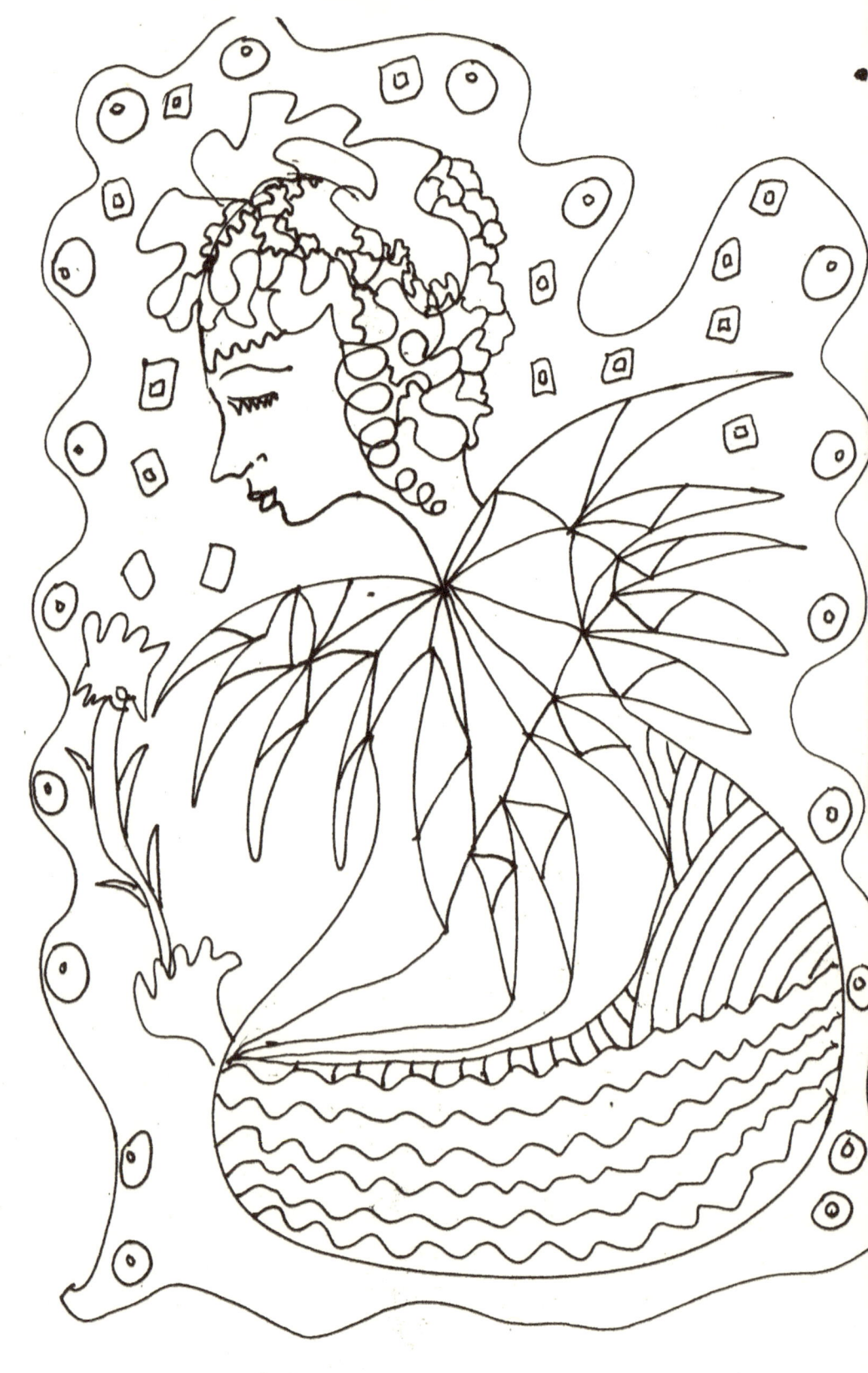

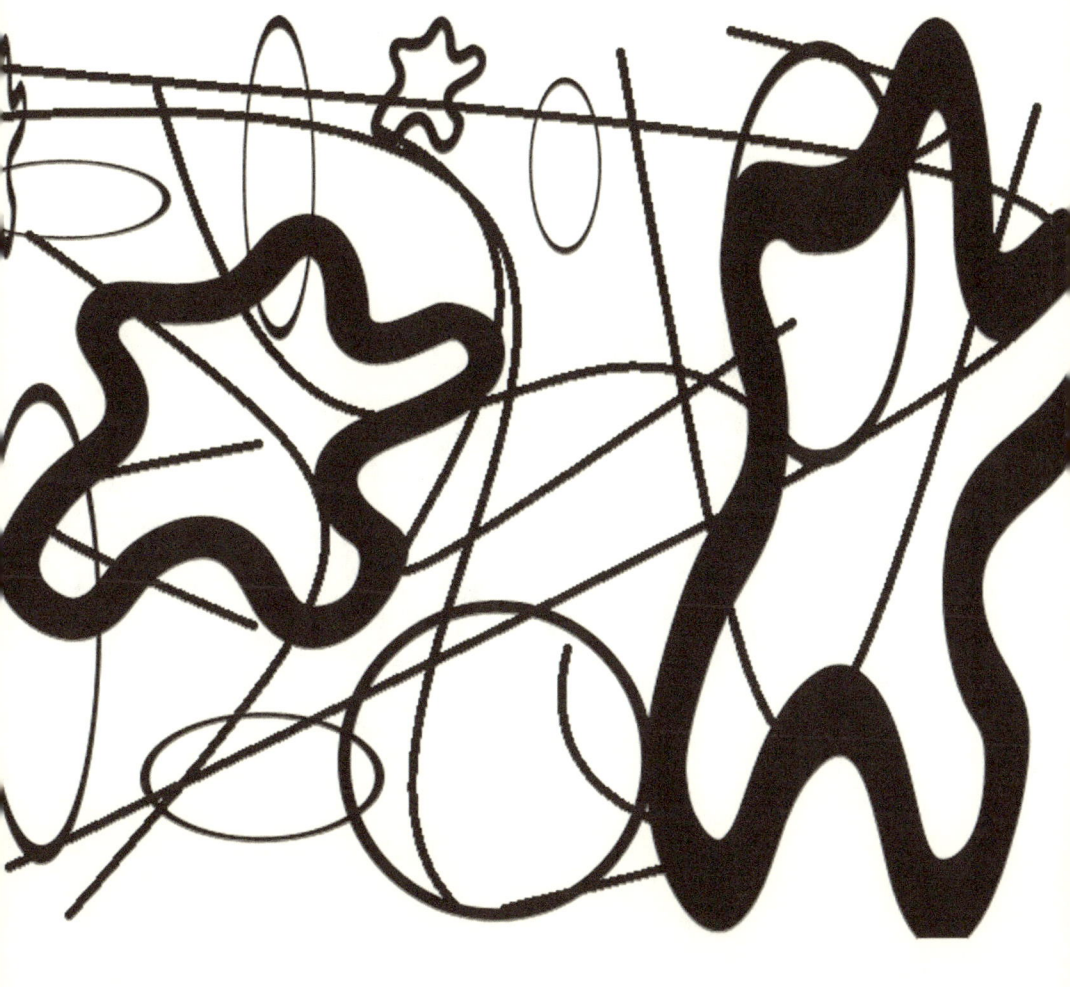

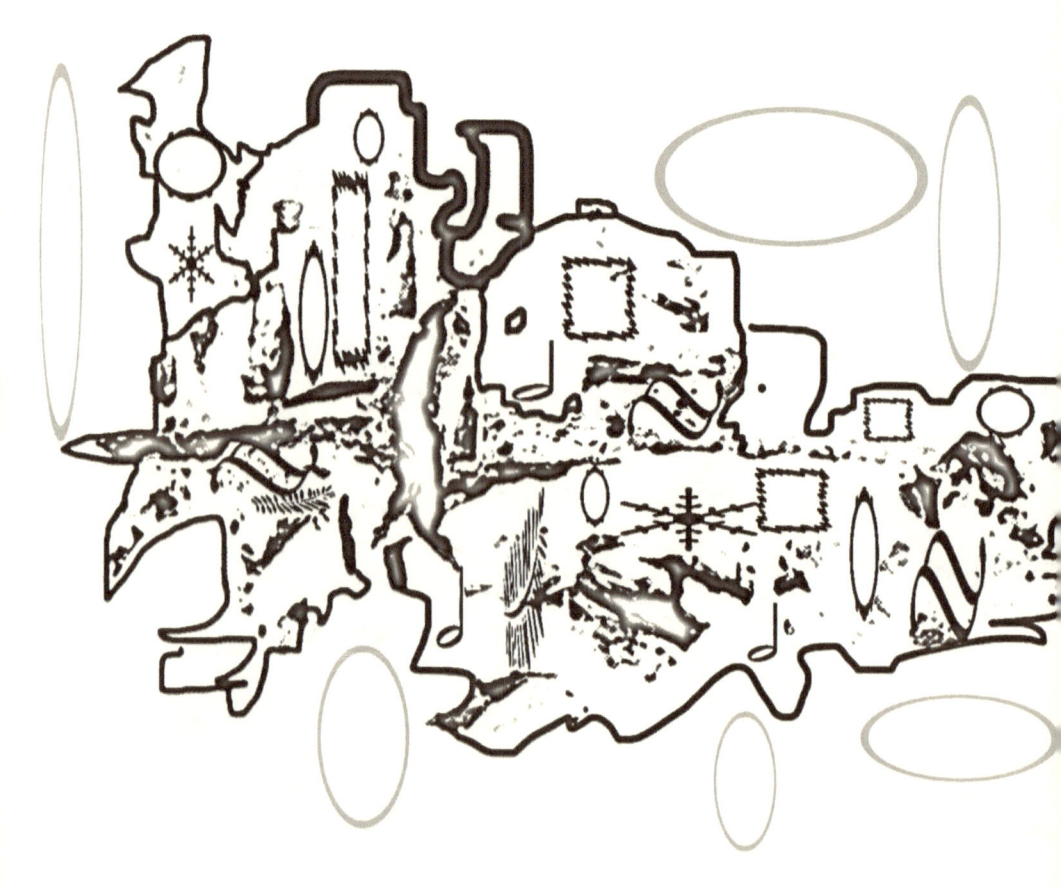

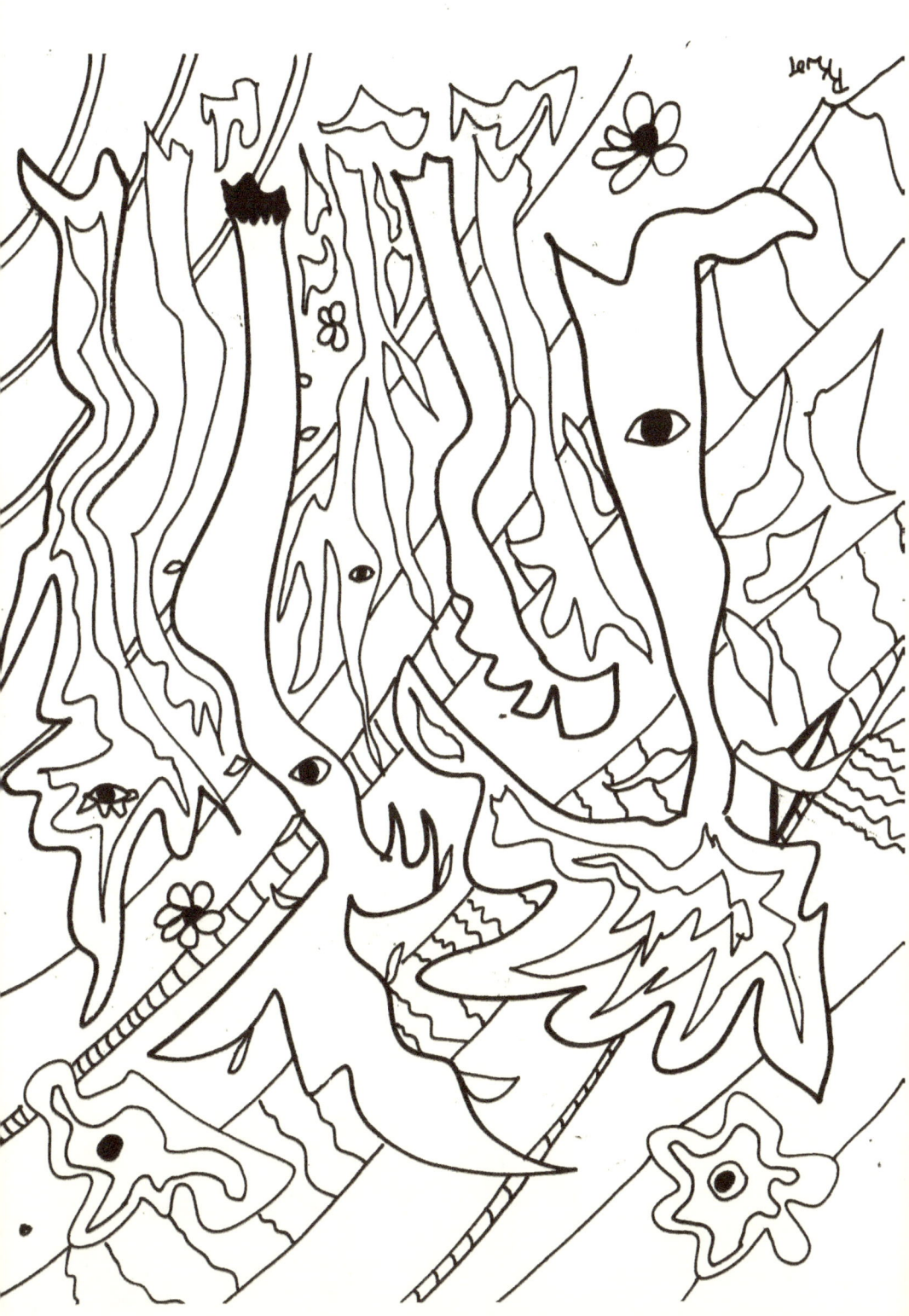

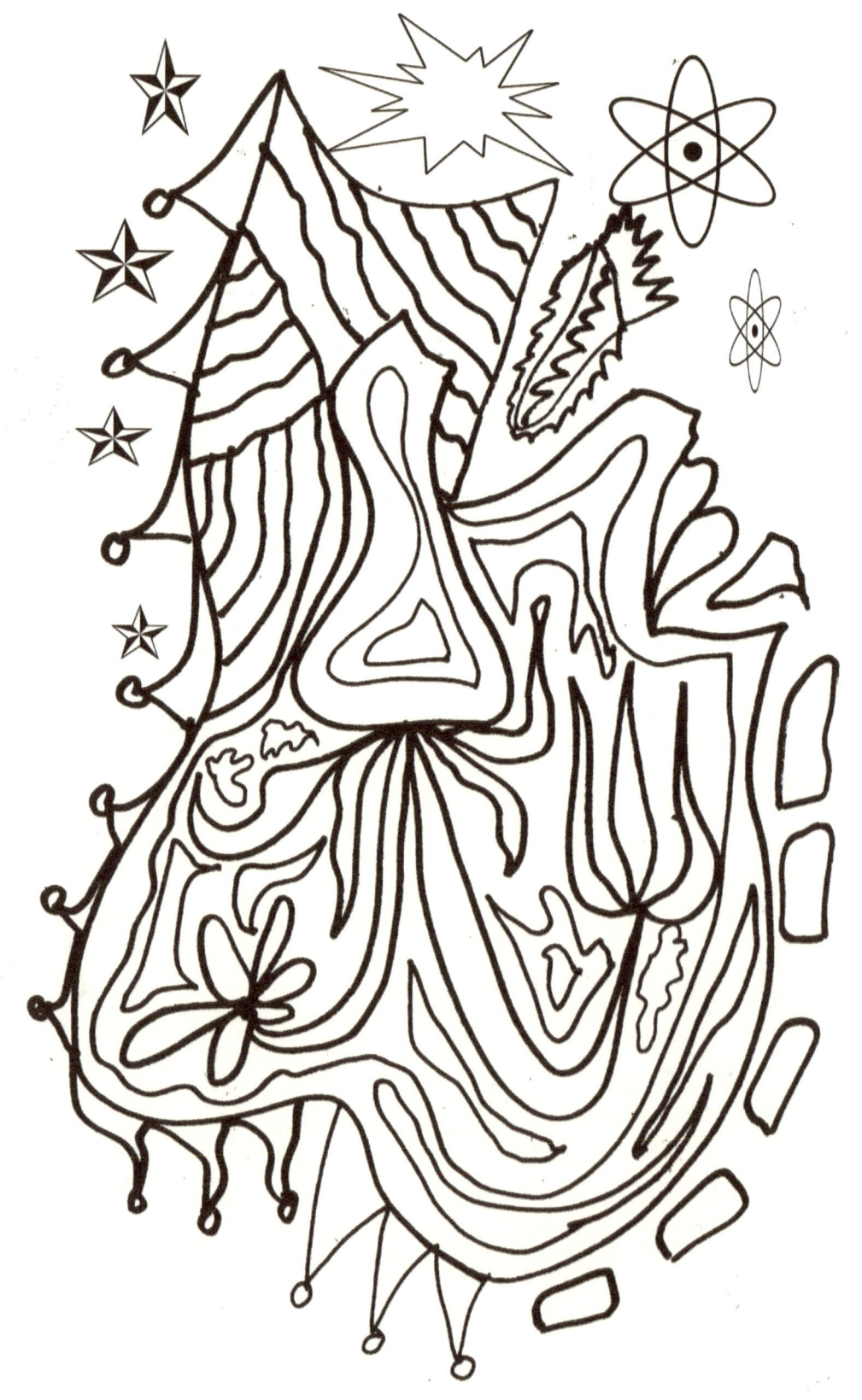

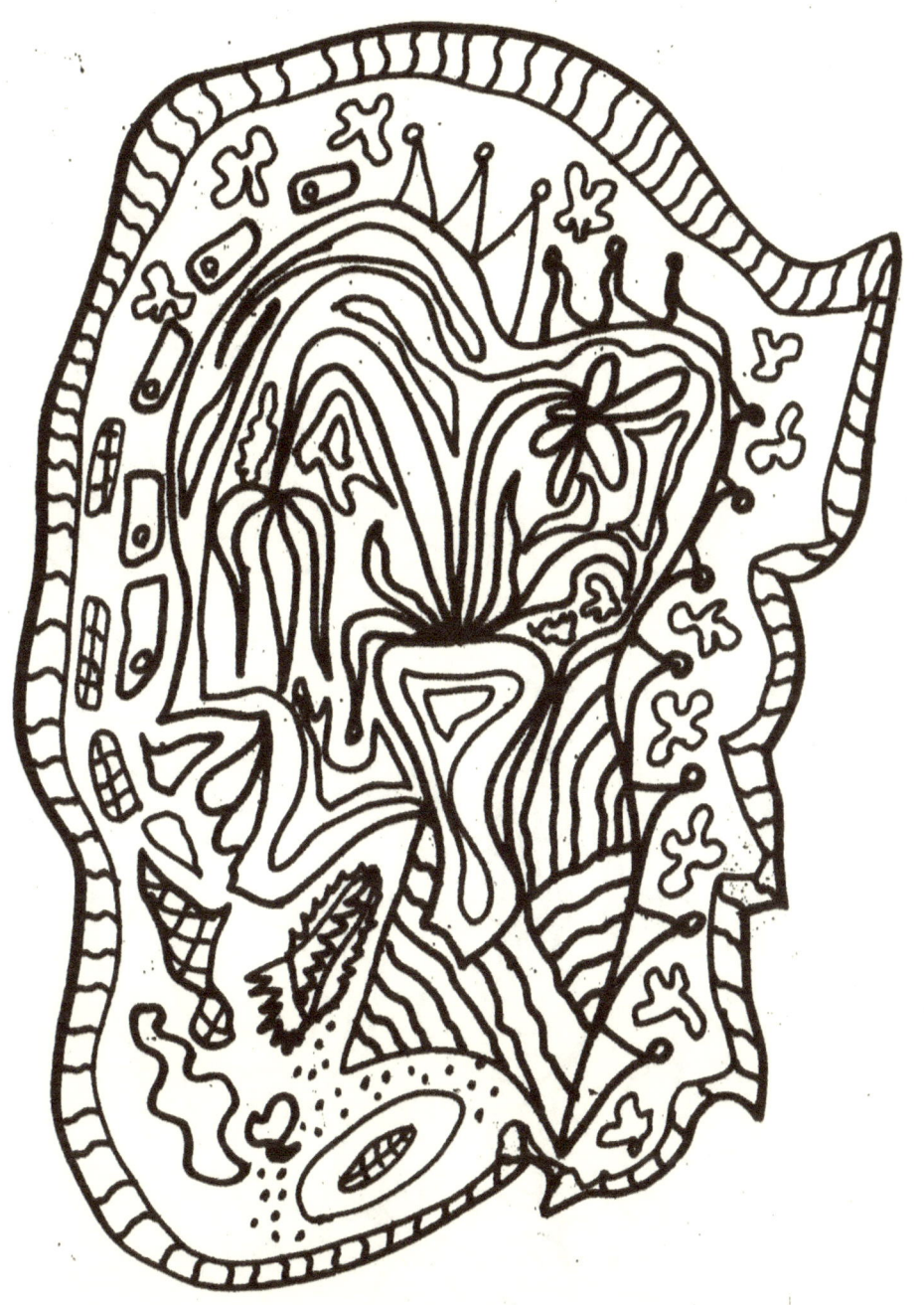

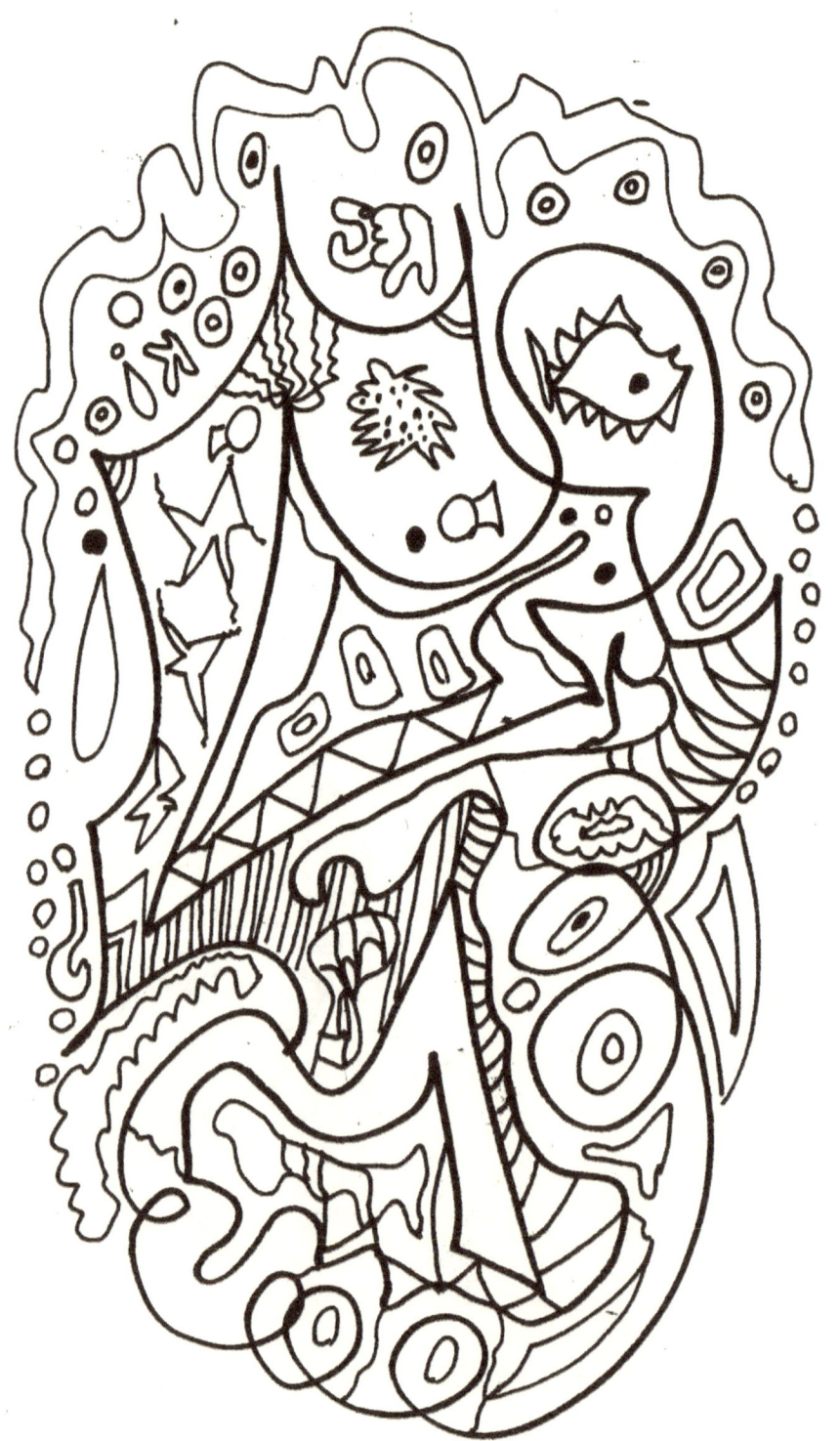

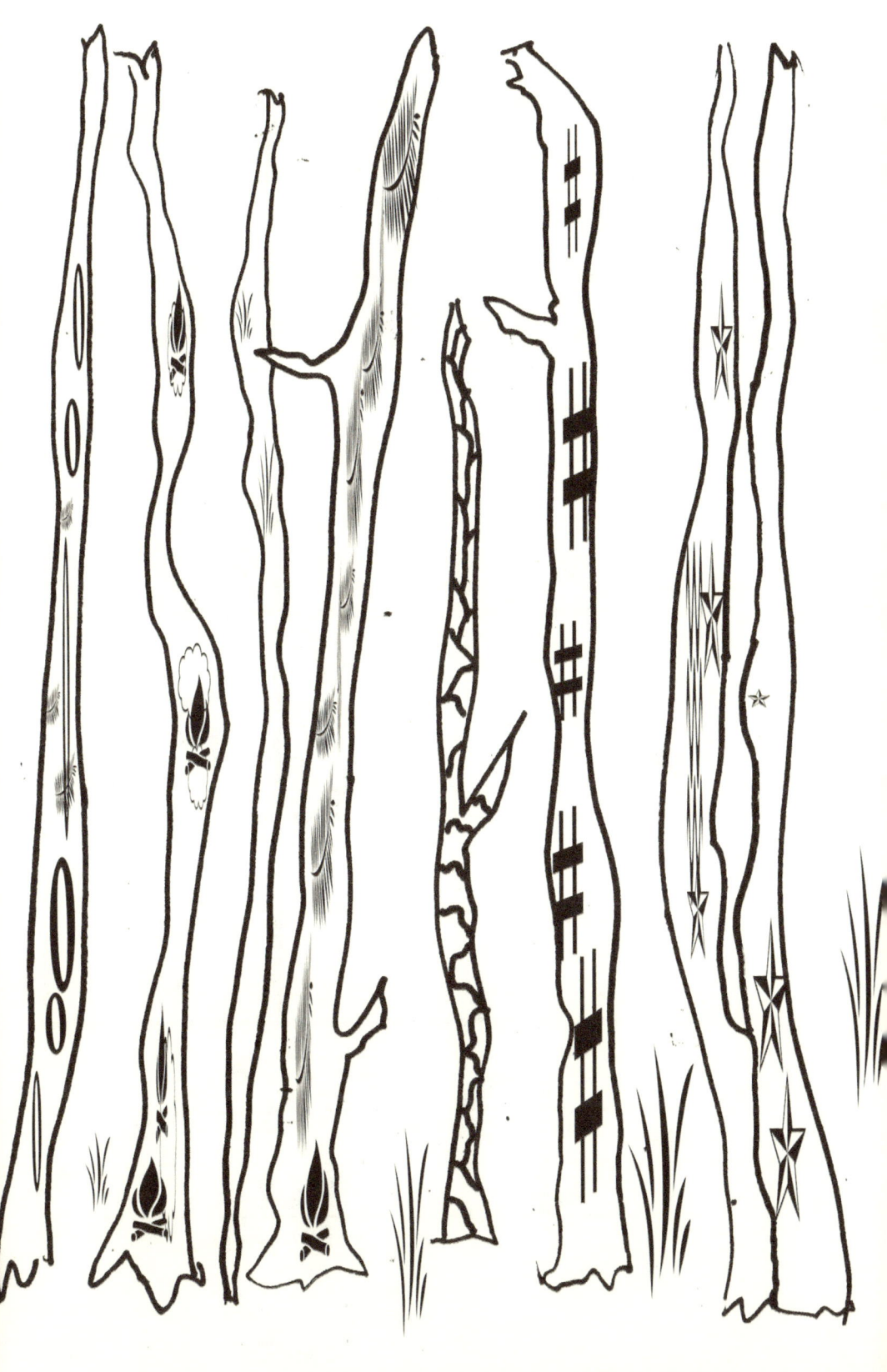

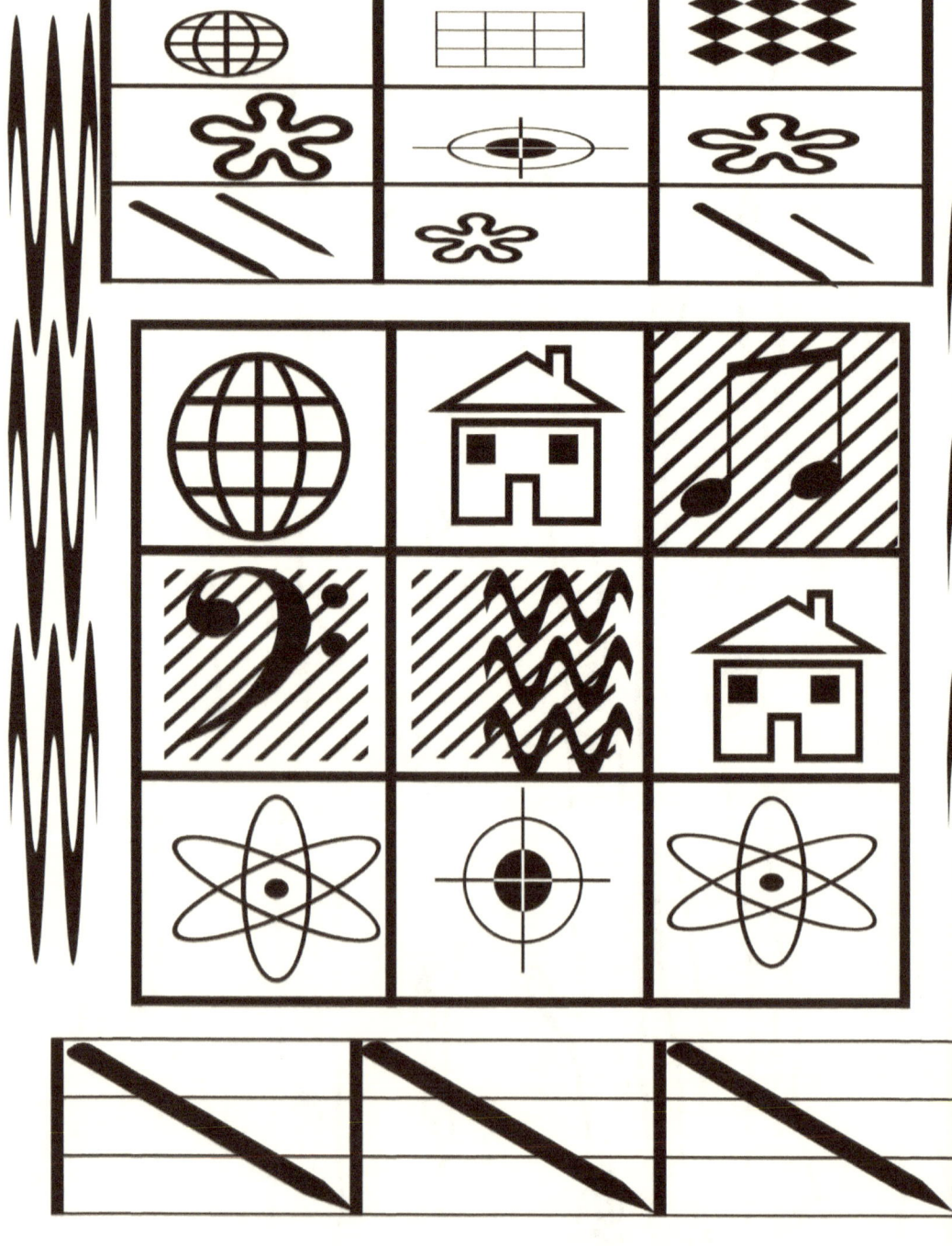

Rosalyn Kliot is an award winning and published artist currently residing in Oregon. Her works have been shown and or sold nationally and in a travelling exhibit in Japan. She has been juried into numerous gallery exhibits in Chicago, Los Angeles, Oregon, Washington, and the Springfield Museum in Oregon. She studied formally, earning a B.A. degree in art while on a full ride scholarship at Roosevelt University. She has also studied with Don and Alice Baum of the Art Institute in Chicago. Her works can be seen on youtube and fineartamerica.com.

PINK COLLAGE PRESS - KLIOT STUDIO

www.ingramcontent.com/pod-product-compliance
Lightning Source LLC
Chambersburg PA
CBHW021850170526
45157CB00006B/2380